NAVIGATING TENURE AND BEYOND

A Guide For Early-Career Faculty

SUNDAR A. CHRISTOPHER

American Meteorological Society

Images reprinted with permission from Jessica Bailer.

Published by the American Meteorological Society
45 Beacon Street, Boston, Massachusetts 02108

Print ISBN: 978-1-944970-43-7
eISBN: 978-1-944970-44-4

The mission of the American Meteorological Society is to advance the atmospheric and related sciences, technologies, applications, and services for the benefit of society. Founded in 1919, the AMS has a membership of more than 13,000 and represents the premier scientific and professional society serving the atmospheric and related sciences. Additional information regarding society activities and membership can be found at www.ametsoc.org.

Library of Congress Cataloging-in-Publication Data

Names: Christopher, Sundar Anand, author. | American Meteorological Society.
Title: Navigating tenure and beyond : a guide for early-career faculty /
   Sundar A. Christopher.
Description: Boston, MA : American Meteorological Society, [2019]
Identifiers: LCCN 2018043627 (print) | LCCN 2018044135 (ebook) | ISBN
   9781944970444 (ebook) | ISBN 9781944970437 (pbk.)
Subjects: LCSH: Meteorology--Vocational guidance. | Career development. |
   Vocational guidance.
Classification: LCC QC869.5 (ebook) | LCC QC869.5 .C47 2019 (print) | DDC
   551.5023--dc23
LC record available at https://lccn.loc.gov/2018043627

Dedicated to those who constantly intercede on my behalf

TABLE OF CONTENTS

PREFACE

First, a huge thank-you to all those who have continued to encourage me to finish this book. To Rita Sutton, who saw two books in me even before I knew I was supposed to write! Thank you for your prophetic voice in my life.

To my editing and creative team, Kristi Caudill for her expert opinion, Jessica Bailer and Cynthia Flint for their creative work on the illustrations, Jennifer Geary for cover art inspirations, and finally Ebony Lollis, who remained steadfast and who worked tirelessly to see this through to the very end. Thank you.

To Crystal Lee, for her patience in sifting through this document. Thank you!

Another huge thanks to my amazing wife, Sheba, and my three kids, Grace, Samuel, and Abigail. This is all for you.

Finally, to my students, who continue to inspire me and remind me daily that I cannot grow weary in doing well. Thank you!

Sundar A. Christopher
Huntsville, AL

INTRODUCTION

Several years have gone by since I wrote my first book for the graduate student. It is based on a sowing-and-reaping paradigm—how to navigate graduate school and prepare for the career beyond. I wrote most of the book while on a research trip to England. A few years later, I found myself, again, in England, same place. Maybe it's the beautiful countryside or the tea? Call it what you may, but I found myself writing the bulk of this book—this time for the early-career professor—on that trip.

I find myself at a unique vantage point at this moment. Having climbed up (labored through?) the ranks from assistant to associate and then to full professor, I subsequently became the chair of a department. To make matters even more interesting, I was appointed as dean of the College of Science at the University of Alabama in Huntsville (UAH) in 2014. In this position, I hear from faculty on various issues at formal and informal venues. However, I am still convinced that, as professors, we need to do a better job of mentoring our students toward successful careers. They will carry the torch forward. Some of you that have taken my Professional Development course or listened to me lecture on this topic at other venues are now professors yourselves. You've asked me repeatedly to write my thoughts and experiences down as a guide for early-career professors. So here it is!

I've made the focus of this book about you—the early-career professor—but empowering your student is an important topic and one that should be taken seriously. I hope that the seasoned and the not-so-seasoned professor will read this book. It may, at least, be an amusing read for the veteran professor! I've written this in a fashion that allows you to simply pick up and read any chapter; it is not pedagogical. Heaven forbid! Even I could not bear to read something like that!

There are three major aspects to this book. The first is that you as an early-career professor are eager to take care of your foremost business—getting tenure. This means the ominous tripartite is staring at you: teaching, research (scholarship), and service. In part one, I've written several chapters that will serve as a guide and interspersed are chapters dealing with the politics of being a professor. In part two, I provide guidelines for empowering your graduate student and building a team that will help you become more successful in research. The final section talks about your life after tenure and what to expect from associate to full professorship. I provide some perspective in terms of becoming an administrator as I wrap up this book. I end the book there because my goal is to write the third book from a department chair's or dean's perspective.

Becoming a mentor to students, especially graduate students, is hard, rewarding, and exciting work. My first book was based on the premise of sowing and reaping: if you sow well then you will reap great benefits in your career. This book is built on the premise of *trust*. I believe that, if a solid trust relationship is built between the adviser and the student, a solid foundation is laid. However, it is up to you to empower students to reach new heights in their careers. Go empower them!

Sundar A. Christopher

MANAGING YOUR BUSINESS
AND REACHING TENURE

1

MANAGING YOUR PERSONAL LIFE

I am sure that when this book comes out I will hear from some reviewer or reader that I am beginning to sound like a "life coach" in this chapter. But I don't know how else to write this section. I am fully convinced that how well you manage your personal life will also determine how well you manage your career as an early-career professor.

The first problematic issue is deciding whether to put career before family. It is up to you if you want to handle life that way, as in the following case. A young professor was married and had a young child. He and his spouse had good jobs on the East Coast. When he interviewed for a job in the Midwest to become an assistant professor, I am sure he felt pure adrenaline. He landed the job and moved there without his spouse and child, and his personal life

and career were thus in direct conflict. This professor repeatedly indicated to me that he could not deal with the long-distance relationship, and his lack of personal life made him that much less productive. After a few years of struggling with maintaining a family long distance, they resolved to be in one place. The entire family is now in the Midwest.

Since I am on the subject of spouses, I've been asked how I would handle things if I were working for my spouse or vice versa. I couldn't handle it. And I probably would not put myself in that situation. The person who asked me that question went on to explain the stress of his spouse working on his team. Dinner conversations were strained, and the pressures of work easily spilled into the home life. My suggestion, since he was the team lead, was to place his spouse in another team. He agreed. The change has since been made and seems to be working!

I hope these examples help you realize that there are many things going on in your career. Therefore, it is important to put your house in order. This book is not written as a fairy tale. I know that there are real threats out there—illness, deaths, accidents, etc. I am not talking about these issues. As I've said in my previous book, when serious issues like these happen, you have to reassess everything—and I mean everything—in your life and figure out what works best for you. For those issues that are merely frustrating but not life changing, however, you have to decide how to quickly address them and maintain stability.

THE TRIPARTITE

I wish someone had given me this piece of advice when I started my career: take care of your body. One of the biggest pieces of advice that I can pass along is to set up a physical exercise regimen early in your career. It is no secret that vigorous physical exercise is exceedingly beneficial for keeping yourself fit. No one ever tells you that professorship is like a marathon. If you do not have good habits set up before your tenure decision year, what makes you think that things will change with time? It is important to clearly mark your calendar each day or several times a week to leave your office to get some exercise. I know of a successful researcher who swims every day during the lunch hour. No appointments are ever made during that time. This keeps him focused and prepared for the long run. I know of another who runs several times a week in the afternoons after he gets home. Rain or shine, the running appointment is kept. I guard my racquetball appointments jealously. Exercise is just one part of the equation.

The other part of this equation is good eating habits. As a young professor, it becomes really important to be more mindful of what you eat. You have to leave behind the three-hamburgers-for-one-dollar days and enter the oatmeal, vegetable, and fruit zone. While I am at it, let me mention water intake as well. Trust me. Keeping a good, consistent, exercise regimen and good eating and hydrating habits will pay off in the long run. I know of some of my colleagues, even while on travel, who lace up their shoes and go running. That's some type of commitment!

The final part is rest and relaxation. Type A personalities and overachievers forget to take a break, rest, and rejuvenate. While I do not consider myself to be either type A or an overachiever, I am guilty of not resting enough or resting well. Resting appropriately is rejuvenating and fires up the research ideas and productivity. Rigorously manage your calendar. You need to be thinking about your summer break during the winter holidays. Write ideas down and take your vacation. You don't have to go on expensive trips; simply finding ways to unwind for a period away from the daily work is important. It takes a few days to even realize that you are on vacation. After that realization, then the vacation actually starts. So, make sure that you carve out adequate time to decompress, and then enjoy the time off. This does not mean that you have to agonize about not answering your emails or checking in. The once-in-a-while check-in is OK. For some of you, being out of touch will drive you crazy. If you need to check in for thirty minutes once a day for your own sanity, do so. But if you do it excessively, it is not a vacation at all! Give yourself an opportunity to take a break and relax. Unplugging every now and then is healthy (and that means turning off your smartphone). You will come back with more enthusiasm for the job.

THE SABBATICAL

As an aside, let me talk a little bit about the sabbatical. Most, if not all, universities offer their faculty members an opportunity to take a sabbatical for an entire year (or part of the year). Surprisingly, most faculty members do not take a sabbatical. A sabbatical for a productive researcher does not have to be a nonproductive time. It can be a time to learn new things in a new environment and come back with fresh ideas, networks, and a brand-new perspective. What exactly is a sabbatical? You are given a year with no teaching responsibilities, and most universities give you half of the pay or some portion of the regular pay. You are expected to supplement the remainder with research funding or with fellowships from the place where you spend the sabbatical. You can pretty much go anywhere in the world, but you must tell the university how it will benefit both you and the university in the long run. If you have been collaborating with teams around the world, here is your chance to pack your bags and leave for a year to work together in person.

The worst thing to do is stay in your office on a sabbatical. You gain nothing—not even rest—by simply not teaching but keeping everything else the same. For some professors, this is their reality. Another issue is that, if your spouse is working, you cannot just ask your spouse to take off for a year. If you have children, then this complicates matters as well. But there are creative ways to navigate family issues. Consider using the sabbatical year to home-school your child in another country. Use the world as a learning place. Get imaginative. I strongly suggest that you leave the country, live abroad, network with researchers, and build collaborations. It's just a year, and it's a fabulous opportunity! You'll thank me for this advice. If you cannot leave the country for whatever reason, at least travel within your current country. Get into a new schedule, learn how others manage research and time, and do some creative research that cannot be done while you are juggling responsibilities at your home institution. This allows you to rest, rejuvenate, work at a different pace and on a different schedule, and do some excellent work. Note that the sabbatical is not a vacation but a time to think outside the box.

I've been asked if I have practiced what I've preached. Always (OK, almost always). I took my one-year sabbatical to Australia. My wife and I sold our home in Alabama, took our three kids (ages 2, 4, and 7), and headed off to Australia. It was daunting in the beginning. But, as always, things work out. We found a good place to live; I walked to work every day, learned how to drive on the other side of the road, bought and sold a car, made some wonderful friends, and even spoke some Aussie. I watched cricket, ate some fantastic ethnic food, traveled quite a bit, and came back home richer for the experience. I wrote some good research papers while I was in Australia, networked well, gave several presentations, and picked some new lines of research work. And, of course, the beaches of Australia were a huge bonus, mate!

TAKE-HOME MESSAGE
Managing your personal life in a way that balances your professional life will allow you to be more productive in your research and have peace at home. Proper time management is key for finding and maintaining balance. It is important to understand that rest is a key component of productivity and must not be sacrificed.

JOURNAL ENTRY

Are there areas in your life that lack balance? Is your personal life being sacrificed for your professional life or vice versa? How might you be able to strike a balance between the two?

FOOD FOR THOUGHT

1. Where would you want to take a sabbatical? How might you be able to make it happen?

2. What physical activity do you enjoy the most? How can you work it in on a daily basis? If there isn't one, how might you be able to fit in a daily walk around the campus during a window in your schedule?

NOTES

MANAGING YOUR TIME

2

Yes, it is true. Time is like money, except that you cannot save time. You lose it rather quickly if you spend it unwisely. The biggest complaint I hear from many young professors is that they are too busy. Too busy! Well, I hear that from the seasoned professors who are not doing much research or who have mastered the art of being deadwood as well. OK, glad I was able to get that out of the way.

I tell my graduate students this: they should expect their advisers to be busy; if not, something is wrong. But there is a difference in being productively busy versus being busy for the sake of being busy. When you are a new or early-career professor, you are trying to work on several things at the same time. Hopefully, you put together a good time-management system while you were in graduate school. If not, you'd better get a system in place. Pronto!

Whether you like it or not, modern methods for managing time—such as online collaborative calendars—are the way to go. Put up a calendar with your schedule on a service such as Google Calendar and share it with your team members (if you have team members). This is an open, transparent way to do business. Of course, you can also manage personal tasks and appointments as part of that calendar system as well. This tells your team what you are up to and where you are at any given time (do not harbor intentions of "I don't want people to know where I am") as well as your travels and your meetings. Your team members can adjust their meetings with you more effectively if they know what you are doing. As an early-career professor, you can give up grand notions of the university giving you a staff assistant to help manage your research and life!

I am not going to talk about short-term, midterm, and long-term plans in this section. Instead, I'll discuss the nuts and bolts of managing your time.

I am a big proponent of having an open office policy. Unless something is absolutely critical in terms of deadline, don't shut your door. A shut door signifies that you are too busy for discussions, let alone mentoring. A student remarked to me that he hardly ever knows if one of his professors is working because his office door is ALWAYS shut. The professor walks into his office in the morning and simply shuts the door. He only comes out for very short periods of time. For a new professor, this is highly detrimental. Word quickly gets around that you are not collegial. Chairs, directors, and deans are not going to provide opportunities for advancement for closed-door professionals.

Mark your calendar with things that happen on a weekly basis. In the semesters that you are teaching, this means courses happen at the same time every week on certain days. Team meetings can be marked as well as individual meetings that happen at the same time each week or at certain time periods. If there are regularly occurring meetings in the department or committees, then those should be added to your calendar, too. (As discussed, remember to block out times for exercise so you can work on your personal health.) Early in your career, resolve to attend meetings at the scheduled times, especially with your students. Nothing panics or disillusions students more than if their professor misses meetings with them. It makes them feel that their work is not important or, worse still, that they are not important! One of the common complaints I hear from students in the Professional Development course that I teach for graduate students is that their advisers are not available or miss scheduled meetings. When you build a team of students and other professionals, how you set the tempo for your team through your actions is how your team will respond.

It is important for you to clearly block off set periods of time when you are not to be disturbed so that you can concentrate on research, proposals, and paper writing. Some of this time can be away from the office as well. I have a colleague at another university who works almost exclusively out of coffee shops. I will admit that I am envious of the fact that he gets to work out of coffee shops! He is extremely productive and his team meetings sometimes happen in these coffee houses. Not all of us can afford that type of flexibility, but it is nevertheless wise to work away from the office at least once a week—safe from daily interruptions—so you can be productive. Some researchers who employ time away from the office often use a library or a quiet place (or not so quiet if it is a coffee shop).

Remember that it is the research that inspired you to get a PhD, develop a team, and become a leading researcher. It is critical that you find time to do your own personal research.

TIPS FOR TIME

Here are some final thoughts for effectively managing your time:

1. Put a system in place. Use a collaborative time-management or calendar tool (e.g., Google Calendar). Provide calendar access to your team to improve transparency and communication.
2. Mark regularly recurring meetings on your calendar, including all teaching and committee meetings.
3. Block off time for your personal research to write papers and proposals, read and review papers and proposals, and analyze data.
4. Have fun with your research and ensure that you allocate time for creative research.
5. Work away from the office for a few hours a week to think in an uninterrupted mode.
6. Stick to your appointments. People will appreciate your promptness.
7. Make sure that you exercise regularly.
8. Remember that you do not have to let the calendar run your life. Impromptu talks and discussions with your team and others are important as well. I certainly enjoy the occasional lunch outing with my colleagues.
9. Adjust your time-management techniques with the stages of your career. If it is working, leave it alone. If it is not, then an overhaul of your time-management strategy may be required.
10. Plan time for some rest and rejuvenation on a regular basis.

At some point, it is possible that someone (administrative staff assistant or student assistant) will help manage your time. If you have a system in place before that happens, you can train that person on how you want your time managed. While there are a plethora of tools currently available, time management is very much like research and teaching. Managing time takes thought, practice, and dedication.

I know a faculty member who is known for his sheer research brilliance, his eccentric way of teaching, and his absolute inability to manage time. To add to this disarray, his office was a sight to behold, with things strewn everywhere. Years ago, I suggested that he hire a student to help him with his daily tasks of filing and organizing items to get him out of the rut of disarray. I even made the effort to find a student to help him. Guess what happened next? Nothing! The faculty member did not know how to organize the disarray and, therefore, was not able to communicate with this student on what steps to take. The student simply sat in her office, and the faculty member went about his usual business of being in disarray. Unless you know how to organize, you cannot communicate to anyone else about how you can be helped.

TAKE-HOME MESSAGE
By managing your time wisely and maintaining a transparent calendar, you will be able to juggle your responsibilities as a professor, mentor, and researcher. Maintain an open office policy and schedule time to work away from the office as well. By doing this, your research will flourish, and the administration will take notice.

JOURNAL ENTRY

Do you need to reexamine the time-management tools you are currently using? Are there time wasters robbing you of valuable research or rest time? For one day, write down how you have spent your time and evaluate how you may be able to improve your time management. Assess whether your time-management tools need tweaking.

FOOD FOR THOUGHT

1. What time wasters are currently eating away at your productivity? What are some steps you can take to eliminate or minimize them?

2. Time management isn't just for work. Have you integrated aspects of your personal life into your time-management system so that you can maintain balance?

NOTES

SETTING GOALS

3

Goal setting is important for your career. Without goals and a vision to meet those goals, it is possible to become chaotic in your approach. Furthermore, goal setting helps minimize wandering aimlessly about in your career with no strategic milestones or ambitions. Goals help you to be proactive rather than reactive in situations and projects.

The first goal of earning tenure is already set for you by the university. I talk about how to work that situation in another chapter, but for now, just know that you can make that decision easier for your university by doing the right things.

So, what goals do you need to set besides earning tenure? I'd be lying to you if I said that I sat down and charted out all my goals when I became a professor. Some things evolve with time, but you must set some goals (if I said "set you must," Yoda fans would be smiling).

RESEARCH GOALS

It is very important to set research goals for yourself. While you may enjoy working in one or two areas, being a university professor is an opportunity to diversify into other areas of research. Your graduate students can be of tremendous help in this regard by doing a lot of the groundwork. (By the way, never ever worry that your graduate student will become your competition after she graduates. If you think that way, you are missing the point of mentoring.) When you received a PhD, you specialized in a certain area of research. Your graduate students will use some of the background you have shared, but it is your responsibility to train them in areas that are reasonably different than yours. They may use the same principles but in a new line of inquiry where they can grow and become successful. This way they are not competition but true future collaborators. I actually tell early-career faculty that it is their responsibility not only to train and mentor their students in their research area of expertise but also to help design a research area where their students can thrive during graduate school and beyond.

There are several types of research goals that you can set, and you can chart them out annually or by three- or five-year periods. Yearly goals should include writing and publishing two or more papers per year for high-quality journals, attending one to two conferences, and speaking at other universities/organizations (invited talks). Three- to five-year goals should range from building a team of two to three graduate students to the addition of research scientists and postdoctoral scholars. You might also have the opportunity to participate in a review paper or collaborate on multi-author papers across the country or internationally.

It is imperative that you set clear goals of how many research papers you will write. This is a good target to communicate to your team so they can strive toward it. As your team grows, the number of papers that you publish each year should increase. Setting these goals helps teams to be productive and efficient in what they do. If you have a good-sized team (we will talk more about building teams later), then think about organizing a special session in a major conference that showcases all your work. That is a worthwhile goal to have.

Another worthwhile goal is to acquire additional funding through proposals. There is nothing wrong in saying that you want to win a certain number of proposals and setting deadlines for those proposals. Growing your team to a desired size and having an appropriate number of graduate students are all useful metrics and goals for producing promising proposals. Although I've never been a proponent of setting funding amounts for your group, you must plan ahead if you have team members who are relying on proposal funding.

TEACHING GOALS

Some argue that it is difficult to put together teaching goals. Although it is true that research goals are a bit easier to form and maintain, it is important to have teaching goals as well. When you started your career as a professor, I assume that the chairperson of your department sat down and discussed teaching assignments and responsibilities. In larger departments, these duties are managed by a committee, and depending upon the number of students, you may end up teaching several courses a year. Research-heavy departments often task their professors with only one course a semester. If you are in a research-intensive department with faculty successful in securing grant and contract funding, you will be expected to do the same. This is the "culture" of that department. If you find yourself not being productive in research, brace yourself for this—you will have to teach more courses per semester. Other departments that have very little research and have primarily a teaching mandate usually task professors with at least two to three courses per term. Therefore, you have to make a decision about your career path and how you want to spend your time. If you enjoy research, then it is important that you find a place that will allow you to teach and do research. Otherwise, you could become frustrated with your career.

Your chairperson should tell you this: it is important that you teach at least one or two courses with large class sizes before your tenure-decision year. Also, make sure that you design new courses or volunteer to teach classes at the undergraduate level (if that is not already an expectation). Give members from other departments in the university no reason to pass you by when your dossier is reviewed. When I have been on promotion committees, even if a faculty member who is going up for promotion has excellent research skills, a few Promotion and Tenure Advisory Committee (PTAC) members complain about certain aspects of teaching (small class sizes, lack of differing topics in courses taught, no undergraduate teaching experience, and the list goes on). Don't give the committee reason to turn you down. Remember that this is the day and age when online learning is ubiquitous. Students take more online courses because of the convenience. As an early-career professor, work your way into online learning if your courses lend themselves to it.

SERVICE GOALS

It is good to put together goals for service as well. Serving on certain committees could bring higher visibility to you and your team. Set your aspirations on national- or international-level committees and give it a go. Work through your networks and place your name in the running to serve on such committees.

As an early-career faculty member, your strategy for serving on committees should be different than veteran faculty. You are often expected to serve on multiple types of committees during the time that it takes for you to become tenured. Just bear down and engage effectively in these committees. I've had my share of serving on parking and commencement committees! Once you have earned tenure, your strategy should change.

CELEBRATE SUCCESS

Celebrating successes and goals reached with your team is equally important. Be sure to maintain a level of enthusiasm among your team. Years ago, I was in a research discussion with a colleague of mine when he suggested that I create a glory board. I had no idea what that meant at the time. He took me near his office and showed me a large board that had all his papers displayed in a nice format. Pictures of his team members, accomplishments, awards, and upcoming events for his team were neatly displayed as well.

I took his advice to heart and placed a board outside my office with similar information. It was a huge success since my team members enjoyed seeing the accomplishments of the team. Every paper published for the year was testimony of our hard work. A surprisingly pleasant by-product was that—since it was in a corridor—as people walked by, everyone had an opportunity to see the progress and accomplishments of our team. Another by-product was that it motivated other faculty members to do better. All in all, it was good advice from my colleague. Some argue that this is what a website is for. While I agree that a website that highlights the team's work and successes is mandatory, having a board outside of an office with the team's accomplishments is more visual and immediate. So, I'll pass along that advice as well. Put together a glory board, place a few posters, and see how it works for the team.

I'll end the section by saying that setting goals is not a one-time event. Rather, it is a process that needs to be written down, adjusted, fine-tuned, and often revisited.

TAKE-HOME MESSAGE

Goal setting is a continual process. It is important to revisit your mid- to long-term goals to evaluate your work in the face of changes within the field. Make sure you establish goals for each section of the trifecta so that you do not neglect or lose passion for what you are doing. Remember that adjusting goals on occasion can bring about more productivity and inspiration.

JOURNAL ENTRY

Write down when you started as an assistant professor. What is your mandatory tenure year? Do you plan to apply for early tenure? If so, when? List reasons why. How many papers do you plan on publishing each year until your tenure year? List your goals of writing proposals. How many graduate students will you employ?

FOOD FOR THOUGHT

What goals would you like to see accomplished, and what is your target date? Think in terms of service, research, teaching, and even leisure.

NOTES

THE INTERVIEW PROCESS FOR EARLY-CAREER FACULTY

4

I've been writing with the approach that you already hold the position of faculty member. Let's backtrack a bit to before you were employed at a university. We can discuss the nerve-wracking application process and the often-intimidating interview process.

No two interviews are the same given the differences among jobs. Every university goes through its own hiring process, but trust me when I say this: several people at the university are involved in posting a job, screening applicants, setting up interviews, and negotiating and writing offer letters. There are many layers of administration for these types of issues. In most universities, lawyers are also involved in writing the offer letters.

Your application for a faculty position needs to be convincing. Think about the perspective of the department that you are applying to when preparing

the material. At minimum, you need a top-notch curriculum vitae (CV) and an impressive cover letter detailing why you think you are a good fit for this position. But allow me to single out the CV. A CV should be formatted so that it is easy to read. Key items of interest should stand out. When considering you for a faculty position, department members will first look for your ability to do research and how successful you have been in research. They will then look for any teaching experience as a graduate student or in other previous positions; some of you have been in postdoctoral positions for a while before deciding to embark on a career as a faculty member. The third qualification is, you guessed it, your service accomplishments in organizations and other venues. If your CV is already strong in these three components (teaching, scholarship/research, service), then your CV is going to rise to the top. To help ensure it stays at the top, another important item to have in a CV is your ability to communicate and work with people. Usually, universities hire you not just for the short term but for the long haul; they want you to be a future leader. Give them reasons to believe in you.

Let me repeat myself by saying that every department is looking for the correct fit for a faculty member. Therefore, if you are applying to a research-intensive department, their method for screening CVs, interviewing, and deciding on related issues will look very different when compared to a department that is more teaching oriented. Do your homework before you apply for these positions, and make sure that your cover letter highlights the necessary details that a CV cannot. If you are primarily interested in a teaching position, make sure that you apply for such positions. Some departments have a high expectation for research, and you want to make sure that your career goals match the department needs.

Typically, departments look for faculty members who have the ability to do great research. This means that they are looking for someone who has already published several peer-reviewed journal papers. If you're reading this book with the aspirations of applying for a faculty position a few years from now, make sure that you publish several high-quality papers. The competition is intense, and you might as well get ready now! Departments also look to see if you have presented your work at conferences. If the department sees you as a strong candidate, you can rest assured that someone from the department will call one of your research colleagues to discuss your research potential, your ability to work with others, and your personality. For those of you who have done some reading on what criteria is used to hire faculty, you may remember KSAO—Knowledge, Skills, Abilities, and Other Traits. Interpersonal skills and your ability to work in a team are important "Other Traits." Therefore, show yourself to be collegial at every phase of your career, and it will do you well in the long run. Your CV will automatically begin its ascent process if you are published. What will quickly get you to the top of that heap is if you had secured some research funding while you were a postdoctoral researcher or if you had written and won proposals as a student. Imagine if you were hiring someone for a faculty position. Wouldn't you be impressed if someone wrote an NSF Graduate Research Fellowship Program (GRFP) proposal and won that award? If you are currently in graduate school, start the proposal writing process now. The more credentials you have under your belt, the better position you will be in when you get to the salary and startup negotiation phase.

Most candidates that I have interviewed state that they have taught undergraduate laboratories while they were graduate teaching assistants (GTAs). That is a good start. Some departments have what is called Supervised Teaching Credits. This is where a faculty member mentors a student to teach several weeks of an undergraduate class. If you can do this while you are in graduate school, consider yourself to be among the select few. I often provide opportunities for my graduate students to review papers alongside me. Yes, I do send a note to the editor getting his or her permission to do so, and I have yet to have an editor say "No." It is a tremendous experience for the student, and I strongly encourage the early-career professor to train students to review and write formal responses. By the way, this definitely falls in the service category.

There are numerous examples of a CV everywhere these days, so I am not going to delve into the building blocks of writing one, but here are some guiding principles:

1. Do not pad your CV. This means, for example, that you should not try to list all of your conference presentations as peer-reviewed work. The people reviewing your CV are experts, and they will see through such chicanery.

2. Do not misrepresent where and how long you have worked and in what capacity. Remember that there will be a background check and a conversation with many references. There is no sense in creating problems for yourself. I once had someone apply for a position who stated that they had received a PhD from a certain university. A quick check revealed that the candidate had never completed a dissertation (the haloed ABD—All But Dissertation).

3. Make sure that you list your education and affiliations in descending order. Most recent job first, please.

4. Needless to say, proofread a few times and have a couple of people look it over for a sanity check.

5. The cover letter should be written to carefully highlight your qualifications and, as previously stated, to explain why you feel you are a good fit for the job. Talk a little about how your research interest dovetails with others in the department. You do not have to necessarily state the names of people. Show your enthusiasm for teaching

and the types of things that you can teach and develop in a teaching portfolio. Research the strategic priorities for that university and then state how you can be a team player and help that plan. End the letter positively. Never be overly aggressive or eager in your cover letter. Learn how to strike a balance.

Recently, I read a very compelling cover letter from a faculty search where the candidate discussed succinctly his eagerness to help students succeed at the highest levels and, therefore, help student retention. He had obviously done his homework by looking through the university web pages that stated increasing retention was an important goal. Well done!

THE HIRING PROCESS

There is a chain of events that takes place after a department receives applications. There is a departmental committee that sorts through the applications and creates (usually) a "yes," "no," and "maybe" stack. If there are many applications in the "yes" stack, the committee will simply not bother to come back to the "maybe" stack.

Once the "yes" stack is sorted, the committee will decide on a small number of applicants (usually fewer than 10) to conduct preliminary interviews with. This could be a phone conversation or videoconference of some kind. It all depends upon who is doing the interviewing.

In your preliminary interview, you need to make sure that you communicate clearly. You might be given a few minutes to talk about why you are interested in the position before they ask you questions. Take notes because there is a good chance that you will be invited to the campus for an interview. Typical questions are always about your research and teaching aspirations or where you see yourself in a few years. The initial interview is to determine how well you communicate. They already know your CV, and now they want to get that first glimpse of you. You do not necessarily have to dress up in a jacket and a tie for a teleconference, but neither should you look unkempt or be in your pajamas. Strike a balance. At the end of the interview—if it is a well-conducted interview—you should be asked if you have questions. Ask the usual questions about the timeline for the process and when you can expect to hear back from them. Overall, it should be a relatively quick phone conversation (unless you have a committee that loves to talk).

Now comes the big part in the process. The committee will deliberate on who to invite to campus for the next interview. Typically, there are three candidates that will be invited and only one chosen for the position. If, for whatever reason (there are indeed a myriad of reasons), the candidate rejects the offer, then the offer is made to one of the other two candidates and so on. If all three do not accept the offer, then the committee will go back to the list to get a few more on campus for interviews. However, unless you have someone working at that university, you will never know if you were the first to be chosen or not. It should not matter to you either way; you got the offer. Be happy!

THE TWO-DAY INTERVIEW

The campus interview is often a two-day process. (They will fly you into town in business class! Just kidding. The cheapest possible fare is the way you will have to go with an airline.) Your day schedule will have meetings with the department chair, the dean, search committee members, individual faculty members, and graduate students. You will also be expected to give a seminar of some kind; some departments get even fancier and ask you to do a "chalk talk," which varies by discipline. Either way, be ready to be exhausted! Here are some pointers for your two-day interview:

1. Do not fly in one hour before the process starts. Get there the previous day and rest well before the process begins. You may have to go out to dinner the very first evening that you are there. So be ready!

2. Dress for the occasion. It shows that you are interested if you wear a jacket and a tie or even a suit to the occasion. The dinner may be a casual event, but even then, resist the urge to show up in shorts. A business-casual attire for dinner is fair. For the two-day interview itself, make sure that you dress appropriately in formal business wear. I recently interviewed someone who came in flip-flops and an open-collar shirt with his sunglasses on top of his head—yes, during his interview—and for crying out loud, I am a dean! He constantly moved his chair back and forth. Needless to say, it was a very distracting interview. If you didn't already guess, he didn't get the job.

3. Let's talk about your seminar, which is open to all faculty and students from across the campus. Your seminar should strive to balance between teaching and showcasing your research talents. Talk about the importance of your research, what you solved, and what papers you published. This is the easy part. It is important that you explain the concepts elegantly in your talk so even someone not in your field will be able to appreciate your work. This sends a clear signal that you are an efficient communicator who will have no problem explaining difficult concepts to your students when you start teaching. The important part in your lecture is to discuss where your future research lies. How will you connect your current work to future ideas? You need to gently insert discussions about which funding agencies will be interested in your work. Also, do not forget to highlight how your

work connects with some of the ongoing work in the department and in the university. If you do this, congratulations! You just gave an amazing presentation that people will be talking about for several weeks to come (OK, I exaggerated a bit there).

4. Your discussion with the department chair should be cordial and comfortable, but do not forget to ask about departmental expectations for reappointments, promotion, tenure, publications, and winning grants and contracts. Ask what teaching loads are like and if there are opportunities for you to "buy out" of courses with research funding. Ask if you will be allocated GTAs at the beginning, and also don't forget to ask for advice. Department chairs love it when early-career faculty "ask" for advice. You may have trouble stopping that conversation.

5. When you talk to faculty, remember that each member will vote for or against you in comparison with the other two candidates that are interviewing. Therefore, make sure that you are ready to delve deep into research discussions. I am sure that some of these faculty members are eager to discuss the politics surrounding the department and the university. They may be just venting, so some of it might not be accurate. Simply listen and move on to the next topic. Never agree or disagree, let alone sympathize with faculty members on their position about a university matter. You are merely interviewing; there is no reason to get mired in politics.

6. Make sure that you are prepared to talk to students—both undergraduate and graduate. In my experience, not many undergraduate students show up for such discussions, but graduate students will. Graduate students have a unique perspective on departmental affairs. Students are excited about faculty members who care about students. Students need mentors, and they will catch on quickly if you are genuine or not. Your passion for research and teaching is what they care about most, and if you have a mentoring tone in your conversations, the graduate students will begin to trust you quickly.

7. Your conversation with the dean is usually big-picture discussions unless your research dovetails with the dean's area of expertise. If not, deans will talk about the strategic plan of the university, the college, enrollment, and a lot of bureaucratic information that you have no interest in at this stage in your career. Hear them out though. If the university is going through anxiety attacks about graduation rates and retention rates, then the dean will want to know how you can help. This is why you should do your homework before you begin the interview process. If you are going to meet the dean after you meet with the department chair, ask the department chair what issues are

important to the college and to the dean. This way you can get at least somewhat mentally prepared. As dean, I get asked the same questions about the strategic vision of the college and where I see the Department of Chemistry headed in the next five years. By carefully asking every person you interview questions, you can begin to construct an idea about the university's areas of interest.

8. The dean of the college is not going to discuss salary or startup with you at this point because the department has not made a recommendation to the dean on their top choice for the job. All candidates must be interviewed first. Save yourself the trouble and do not get into salary or startup discussions.

9. Now for day two of dinner: A second set of faculty members are trying to figure you out as a person over dinner. You may get interesting questions such as marital status (of course in subtle ways), children, and other personal things. Be careful about oversharing. Be polite but not guarded and stuffy. Be careful about ordering alcoholic beverages. It might get that tongue of yours talking about things that you would not be discussing had you been drinking water or lemonade. I have seen firsthand a candidate loosening up a bit too much in a dinner setting after a few glasses of wine. The chuckles became loud laughter. The speech became a bit slurred, and there was too much oversharing of personal details. Some departments may take you to a local brewery; if you do not drink alcoholic beverages, it is OK to order a nonalcoholic beverage.

10. After a grueling two days, you will get on a plane and head back home exhausted but having learned a lot about another organization. More importantly, you have learned the art of interviewing. With every interview, you will get more and more comfortable and stronger in your discussions with people.

It is a nice gesture to send a note to the chair of the department and the search committee and thank them for hosting you.

THE OFFER AND STARTUPS

The next big step is when you get a call from the university making you a verbal offer. It could be the department chair or the dean or someone else in the university who has been designated to make offers. Typically, there are three things that will be discussed:

1. The salary: Remember that you will be quoted a 9-month salary. Do your homework on salary before you start negotiations. You do not

have to start negotiating in the first phone call. You can get all the information in that first conversation, ask a few questions, and inform the dean (or whomever) that you will reply soon with responses. Make sure that you do not take too much time. If you do not like the terms of the final offer, the university will want to move ahead with making an offer to the next person. (On some university websites you can glean information about salaries. You can also look up other organizations that provide some salary benchmarking information. Either way, you need to be fully prepared if you want to ask for more salary.)

2. A startup package: You will be offered either a salary number or a salary range for you to fit your startup request. Remember that your startup package is to help invigorate your research so you can begin to write proposals and secure extramural funding. Once you arrive at the university, you will be expected to use these funds to add momentum to your research. Holding on to these funds for many years is counterproductive. In some cases, you will be given a blank slate and asked what you expect as a startup package. A good strategy is to state that you have been working through some numbers and that you will provide a detailed answer via email as a spreadsheet in one to two days. Ask the person on the other end of the phone if one to two days is reasonable. Be prepared to work through your startup carefully with justification. Be reasonable. You can ask for lab equipment, chemicals, supplies, graduate students, computers, etc. The list is endless but you need to justify each item with how it will make everyone's job easier. When you send in the spreadsheet, you may be asked to split the startup into year 1 and year 2 costs. Be prepared to scale down your startup requests since not all universities have deep pockets to fund high requests. At some point, if you've reached an impasse in the negotiation, then part ways amicably. Never come across as being arrogant when negotiating salary and startup. Be polite and respectful. Remember that this is a process.

3. Moving costs: It depends on where you are moving from and what you are moving. You can always get an independent quote later and provide those details and negotiate via email. In some universities, these costs are fixed based on your rank and the city that you are moving from. Moving costs should not be deal breakers.

Questions that sometimes do not get asked:

1. What course release will be given during the first year?
2. How many courses will you have to teach per semester?
3. What lab space will you be assigned?

4. How will office space be provided for graduate students working on your research?
5. How long can you keep your startup funds?
6. What about patents and intellectual property rights if your research areas fall into those categories?
7. Is it possible to start during the summer rather than in the fall? If yes, can your startup funds be allocated early in the summer so you can set up your laboratory and begin recruiting students to your lab?
8. Will the department pay for another visit to the university so you can get a feel for your fellow faculty, housing, office, lab space, and the surroundings?
9. Are there internal proposal opportunities for new faculty members?

Once you have settled on all the terms and agreements, you will be mailed an offer letter that you need to carefully read. Sign the letter and send it back to the university. Now you are ready to begin your journey. But wait! Don't forget to go out and celebrate big time with family and friends.

I realize that there are many things that need to be ironed out before you set sail (or drive) to your new university. You may have to wrap up a lease, sell a home, call the movers, and do all the little things that make the list seem endless. Consider this part of the process. No one ever enjoys the process, but at least you have achieved your first milestone on your journey into a faculty position. The best advice I can give you is to prepare for all of this in advance the best you can and then simply go with the flow.

It's normal for contracts to start in the fall semester, but if you can get there a few months earlier, you can get settled in and better navigate your new environment. Your offer letter will give you a date by which you have to report to the department chair. Hopefully from the time you accepted the offer to the time you arrive on campus, you have kept in touch with the faculty.

ORIENTATION

Wherever you land, you will probably be asked to go through an extensive one- or two-day orientation. Universities seem to believe that they need to bombard you with information on the very first week you arrive—a few days before classes start. So buckle up. While your mind is still wandering about and you are trying to get your housing arranged and utilities set up, university administrators provide you with folders and endless PowerPoints on how to get tenure, how to help students succeed, resources available, and Title IX issues. And to top it off, the police chief on campus may talk about campus safety issues. Hang in there! Most of us have gone through these orientation sessions and have survived (although we still have scars).

The most important part of orientation is the human resource aspect. Pay very close attention when you meet with them because it involves money, retirement, direct deposits, how often you get paid, etc. Pay special attention to how retirement is set up. Many places will match a portion of pretax contributions only if you contribute. If they match 5% of your contributions, you will be unwise if you do not avail yourself of this opportunity; it is free money that you are not taking. You will be surprised how quickly time runs away and retirement planning starts. Here's another piece of advice: find a senior professor in the department and talk to them about retirement funds and how your university handles them; they will be eager to share all their expertise and insights.

In short, get through orientation, collect all the material, and go home. You need to rest a day after this information dump!

As I conclude this chapter, let me leave some thoughts behind that will be useful for an early-career professor. Once you arrive at your university and the semester begins, you may have teaching responsibilities (or a release from teaching that first semester) and research and service expectations. Move through all of this systematically. Do not get overwhelmed with too many things at one time. Tackle problems methodically, manage your time wisely, and most importantly, get excited about all the possibilities in front of you.

Make sure that you meet with your department chair at least twice a semester to talk about how you are progressing. Hopefully your department has a mentor assigned to you that you can regularly visit for more of the day-to-day questions. Do not hesitate to send an email to your dean to request an appointment. I suggest doing this once a year. Provide some updates and ask for advice. It is good to engage with academic administrators regularly. When I was an assistant professor, I always sent a holiday greeting before I left for the December holidays, and in that email I highlighted my accomplishments. I sent this to the department chair, dean, and the director of the Research Center that I was part of. I was able to share a bit of my holiday spirit in conjunction with my professional productivity.

TAKE-HOME MESSAGE
In summary, you finished your dissertation, wrote some excellent papers along the way, applied for a few jobs, and landed your first job. Hopefully you negotiated skillfully for your salary, startup, and moving costs as well. Now it is time for you to move from your current location to your new university (moving early is advisable since it will give you some time to prepare and get ready for the fall semester).

JOURNAL ENTRY

The interview process can seem overwhelming and off-putting. One way to make it not so intimidating is to practice and practice some more. Ask a friend or someone you respect to engage in mock interviews with you. Or look online for workshops in your area; they are usually free and open to the public. Write out various questions and scenarios and explore them.

FOOD FOR THOUGHT

I know of a faculty member who negotiated using her startup to pay herself the summer before classes started, came early, set up her office and her lab, recruited students, met all the key people on campus, and started preparing for her first proposal. Not bad for an early-career faculty member! You don't have to do things exactly as she did, but it doesn't hurt to be proactive.

NOTES

THE FIRST PAPER

5

Let's resume where we left off with setting goals. One of your first goals should be getting your research team to write their first peer-reviewed paper.

Often, I give two talks when I travel to universities. The first one is for the researchers and the general audiences alike. That talk is on my research. The second talk, usually in the afternoon in a relaxed setting, is my Professional Development talk. I let the host know that I want only students in that session, but that rarely happens. An occasional professor or researcher would walk in. A few years ago, I was at a major university to give my talk to the students. Lo and behold, I saw an almost bald, graying, well-known professor in the audience. There were about 25 or so students. I kept asking myself, "Why in

the world would a seasoned professor like this want to attend such a talk? Amusement, perhaps?"

Anyway, I started my talk, and every so often, I would emphasize the concept of students becoming proactive in writing papers. I went through a whole slew of topics from managing time and managing advisers to effective communication and remaining proactive in their graduate school days—sow well to reap big later. The talk was over. I entertained a few questions, and then the seasoned professor stood up (cue dramatic music) and said, "Professor Christopher, if I could sum up your talk in one phrase, it would be 'write your papers.'" I did not interrupt, so he continued and said "If a student writes papers at regular intervals, then it means that they are doing all the other things that you mentioned in your talk well." (He mentioned time management and project management, but nothing about managing your adviser!) I nodded and finished the session by saying, "I could not agree with you more!"

STARTING THE PAPER

Writing peer-reviewed papers should be at the heart of every researcher's work—especially if the research has been funded through competitive means (grant/contract). I cannot think of any excuse as to why a researcher would not write peer-reviewed papers. This is a good metric for productivity and shows how tax dollars are being used (most funded research by government agencies is funded through tax dollars). Like the seasoned professor said, it shows that all things are working well in the graduate student's research life. With that introduction, let me provide some guidelines for motivating your student to write that first paper and how to work through the process. Again, this is not a recipe of any sort. The steps taken depend on the student, the research topic, and other considerations. But for most cases, these general guidelines should suffice.

If writing papers is critical to both your team and your research field, then you as the team lead should communicate this regularly and follow through on these issues. For those with teams ranging from five to ten members, it is also a good idea to sit down at the beginning of the year and come up with titles and outlines for the various papers that will be written. Then at a group meeting, it is important to let team members know how many papers will be submitted for that year. This provides a target to work toward. I usually do not worry about when the papers get published. There are lag times between time of submission to the review process and then to the publication process. As long as it gets submitted, I count that as a target. At every group meeting, it is important to review whether the team is on target and what the major stumbling blocks appear to be. Remember, group meetings don't take the place of the valuable one-on-one meetings with your students.

Most students should be encouraged to start writing their first papers after two semesters, usually during the first summer that they are in graduate school. This generally works for the slightly mature graduate student who writes reasonably well and who does not struggle with computer or lab-related issues. The summer semesters in graduate school are typically free of courses so that students can concentrate on research. You as the mentor need to set the tone for this aspect of your students' careers early on . . . the right way.

Here is a sad story. I recently met with a student who had been working on his PhD program for nearly four years. His adviser was brilliant at conceiving ideas, writing proposals, and writing papers. The student had been told to write a paper based on his research. The student was frustrated because every version of the paper that he sent the adviser was sent back via email indicating that it was not good. I asked the student if he was ever taught or given guidelines on how to construct a paper. He said that he was not. Interestingly enough, a week later I ran across his adviser and the discussions came around to the student. The adviser mentioned his struggles with the student and how he was frustrated by the student's inability to construct a paper. I usually do not "tell" faculty what to do, but I suggested that he actually sit down with the student and show him in a step-by-step manner how to write a paper. Unfortunately, this was done three years late. Nonetheless, it seems to be working now, and the student has since published two papers.

In short, it is your responsibility to show students how to write papers. Students usually do not have much experience in writing papers for peer-reviewed publications. They do not know how many figures or tables to place in the paper or how to present the analysis. It is also not a good practice to say, "Read this paper and write your paper like that." I would not recommend that approach as a training method because students are merely emulating someone else's style rather than processing and producing their own style. They are not learning the nuts and bolts of research and writing. You have the experience of writing papers, so it is up to you to help your students gain those skills as well. However, I do recommend continually challenging students to do better literature reviews. This will force them to read relevant papers so they can make good cases for the papers that they are writing.

There are several ways of training students to write good papers. It is important to sit down with the student and actively determine the main theme of the paper and how to best present the results. Some students prefer working with an outline, followed by preparing the figures and tables, and then writing the first draft of the paper. Other students want to write the entire draft since it gives them a sense of accomplishment. Either way, it is important to sit down and decide how to write the paper and what to put in it before the paper is underway.

I'll offer a quick tip for motivating students who may be procrastinating. I often email a title and a quick outline to the students and ask them to start filling in the details. I want the students to write the entire paper (title, abstract, introduction, data, methods, results, and conclusions with figures/tables and references). This will indicate both the length of the manuscript and the scope. The piecemeal method of writing the introduction first and editing it followed by working the next sections rarely works because the students do not see the entire scope and purpose of the paper. Let them write the whole thing out.

Remember that the process of writing a paper is difficult for students, so they need encouragement to finish the process. They have to manage life, course work (if any), and all the other challenges. Writing is not easy for most people. Understanding this fact can make you a better mentor (putting yourself in your student's shoes). Therefore, set realistic time frames on when you want the paper to be sent out for review and work backward to set specific deadlines for the first draft, second draft, and so on.

Make it absolutely clear at the beginning of the process that you expect high-quality results but that you are also there to guide them in that process. Getting students to write the first draft of the *first* paper is, therefore, a critical task and will set the tone for students' research in graduate school. If you have succeeded in doing this, then you can give yourself a pat on the back. Remember that the student knows how to work with data or models and wants to present thirty-five different figures and tables. It is your job to help the student condense and refine all that information into a nice journal paper.

THE DOS AND DON'TS

The next part of the process is probably the trickiest and, for some professors, the most difficult. They look at the first draft and are appalled at the quality of writing, analysis, and everything in between. They have several options.

The Back Burner

"I am so frustrated that I am going to place the paper on the back burner for a while and ask the student to keep doing research. We will write the paper later." This is probably the worst thing to do—especially if the professor does not tell the student why the paper is being shelved. The student is bewildered; therefore, her progress is stunted. The enthusiasm is lost, and needless to say, productivity goes down. This student will not take ownership of this project for a long time, if ever. The adviser has totally demoralized the student.

Bleed Red

"I am going to edit and write in red all over this paper so the student can rework this and send it back." Seeing a million edits on a paper that the student has been working on for a while is equally demoralizing, but at least the student knows what to do now. Some students do not mind this approach, but others take offense to this secretly while they keep working toward submitting the paper.

No Feedback

"I am going to take a while to edit the paper since I am very busy." The student receives no feedback, and the professor gets busier and busier every day. Often, the student does not ask the professor about the status of this paper, or if he does, he gets the response, "Soon." The student loses interest and loses focus on his research. This is often the case as the busyness of new professors meets the inexperience of students' writing. As a result, the whole project is stalled. A paper languishing in someone's email inbox or computer is as good as it being in a trash container somewhere. Therefore, as an adviser, if you want your student to write a paper and if they have given you a draft, then it is up to you to keep the ball rolling.

Multiple Drafts and Quick Turnaround

The last approach often works best and is done in stages. Realize that no paper is ever perfect in the first draft. When you receive a paper from your student, make it your first priority to give your first edits back quickly. By this I mean within two to three days. This maintains momentum and excitement. Work through the entire paper and make sure that the theme of the paper is correct. Revise the big issues first and send it back with some minor edits on top of that. If the sentence structure is not adequate, send it back with some general notes rather than correcting every single sentence. With every iteration between you and the student, work from larger conceptual details to the finer points of sentence structure until you are satisfied with the product. This phased approach appears to be a good strategy when working with students who are in the early stages of graduate school. Plus, each iteration gives them an opportunity to think about their results a bit more.

Let me quickly summarize by repeating that the first paper is critical. The more papers your students are trained to write, the better your team will be, and the happier you will be. However, you must write proposals as well as papers. I often hear that it is not possible to write proposals in some disciplines or that it is not easy to win proposals or… pick your excuse. Writing papers or having grand thoughts about doing research without writing a proposal is downright irresponsible for a faculty member. Some argue that the university must provide support for faculty to hire graduate students to do research with them. Not all universities can and not all universities will. You must have discipline when it comes to writing proposals. There are numerous agencies that will review your proposals. It is your responsibility to start early and write several proposals to establish a track record of winning proposals. I hardly offer a sympathetic ear to those who lament about their win rates for proposals being low. Here is a conversation I had with a faculty member (FM) about his disdain for proposals:

ME: How is research going these days?

FM: Good, I guess; I just wrote a paper.

ME: Congratulations. When are you going to submit that proposal that we have been talking about?

FM: I don't want to submit proposals....

ME: How come?

FM: I hear that the probability of winning is less than 10%.

ME: I get that, but it is important to keep trying. Don't you think?

FM: It is disheartening to see rejection letters from funding agencies.

ME: Can't hit unless you swing. Right? How else are you going to support graduate students?

FM: The university should give me money to hire graduate students to do research.

ME: I would not hold my breath if I were you when it comes to getting graduate student support from the university.

I hope you are getting the point of this conversation. It is absolutely imperative that you write proposals, not just for yourself, but to fund students and then mentor them to success.

TAKE-HOME MESSAGE

For the health and growth of both your research and your team, it is crucial that you establish a paper-writing and publication schedule and goal. Understand that part of your position as a team lead and professor is guiding your students through the writing process and understanding that it can be a very challenging endeavor. Just as you are pushing your students to write papers, you need to actively apply yourself to the writing of proposals. This is not optional. You need to be proactive in obtaining funding.

JOURNAL ENTRY

How do you currently approach the paper publication process with your students? Does your team have set goals, or are they floating rudderless? Brainstorm ways that you can improve your team's publication process today, and then brainstorm incremental steps that you can take to increase both the number and the quality of papers in the near future.

How are you doing with the proposal writing process? Is it a process that you have integrated into your schedule, and have you set a number of proposals as part of your short-term goals? Is this a change that you need to apply to both your goals and your schedule?

FOOD FOR THOUGHT

Great publications are the result of solid guidance and active engagement with the writing process. Writing does not come naturally to most people. Therefore, remember that it is a learned skill.

NOTES

NAVIGATING THE POLITICS OF YOUR DEPARTMENT

6

Having served as department chair for four years and now starting my fifth year of my deanship at UAH, I often encounter many early-career faculty (notice I did not say young faculty) who are trying to juggle their academic and personal lives around the holy grail of tenure. However, this section is not about tenure but about the tangential and mostly neglected topic of department politics. As an early-career faculty member, if you have not encountered department politics such as a cantankerous department chair, an ugly faculty meeting, an obnoxious faculty member, or a jealous colleague, consider yourself lucky. I have encountered a range of situations,

and I have learned how to navigate these thorny issues, often without help. It is impossible for me to know what "politics" you might go through, but I hear from early-career faculty, often when I travel, about these challenging issues.

I still remember this like yesterday. A senior faculty member walked into my office, started a conversation in a benign fashion, and became rude when I did not agree with him. He raised his voice, banged his fist on my table to make a point and to intimidate me, and then stormed out of my office. That was a long time ago when I was a junior faculty member, but it is still freshly etched in my memory. With this preface, here are some guidelines:

1. Remember that you are an early-career faculty member, and your number one priority is to focus on your teaching and research portfolio with adequate levels of service commitments. No matter how great your department, there are always some underlying tensions and issues. Do not get embroiled in any of them. You need to set the tone very early in your career. When you first walk in to the department as a new hire, everyone is eager to meet you, involve you in research activities, show you around, and even share some best practices in teaching. When the "newness" wears off, some faculty members may try to involve you in department politics. You need to politely but firmly indicate that, while these issues are important, you are too new and would rather not engage in these conversations. You need to reserve the right to figure out each faculty member for yourself and not listen to faculty member A's opinion of faculty member B. That's politics. Do not get trapped in this web.

2. Keep your distance. In your eagerness to fit in, do not try to socialize with your fellow faculty and staff members too quickly (and too much). It will make it impossible to untangle yourself when the politics in your department hit hard.

3. As an early-career faculty member, make sure that you attend faculty meetings, take notes, and learn from the dynamics and interactions among faculty members. There are bound to be many matters that will be contentious. For example, how to spend the research budget may be hotly contested. Or, better still, there may be disagreement about which thematic area a new faculty member should be hired for. In all of these cases, take notes and only weigh in if you truly know what is going on. Never take sides just because someone cajoled or coerced you. If you do not know the entire picture, you can simply abstain from voting. The worst thing you could do for your credibility is vote yes (or no) for a certain topic when everyone in the room knows that you have no idea about the complete situation. Never be coerced into casting a vote at a departmental meeting.

4. Trust me when I say this, you will—and I mean you *will*—encounter this following situation: In comes a senior faculty member who is frustrated about a certain departmental/university situation. He enters your office, shuts the door, and then proceeds to rant and rave about his frustrations. If you let it go on too long, this session could go on for hours. In his frustration, he could knowingly or unknowingly speak ill about other faculty members, staff, or administrators. While an hour or two has gone without you saying a word, you realize that you are now trapped in your colleague's web. You must be wise to these situations. Oftentimes, these are faculty members who have already earned tenure and who are set in their careers. They do not care about your aspirations or struggles. They have found someone to listen to them vent. If you have allowed this to happen, there is nothing you can do about it, but you can prevent this from happening again. The next time they walk in and shut the door, politely but firmly draw some boundaries in the relationship. Tell them that you are not ready to assimilate all of the departmental politics and that you are really busy and cannot afford the time. If they still persist, politely stand up, walk toward the door, and encourage them to leave. Do this once or twice and they will get the message.

5. The bottom line to all politics is this: Early in your entry point into the department, clearly send the message that you will not engage in conversations that are unprofessional about other faculty members. It does not matter who is right or who is wrong; you deserve the opportunity to figure out the department for yourself. Ignore the politics and follow up with solid research and impressive teaching portfolios. Write your papers, talk about your research, and drown the negative voices with the upbeat nature of your career. Take charge. That is my ultimate message.

WHAT I CALL POLITICS

Recently, I received two different phone calls. The first one was from a young professor who was frustrated because his department was giving him the cold shoulder when it came to serving on important departmental committees. He was one of the research hotshots in his department, but the chair was not selecting the young professor to serve on committees that would shape the future of the department. The professor lamented that others were being put ahead of him. In his mind, this was department politics.

The next call was rather interesting. This young professor had recently won several grants and was quickly garnering recognition for his leading-edge work. He was a recent hire in the department, and one of the seasoned veteran researchers was consistently avoiding collaboration with him. The veteran researcher was extremely successful. When it came to writing omnibus proposals, the young professor was given a cold shoulder. To make matters worse, for whatever reason, the veteran researcher appeared to pick other scientists for collaboration. The young professor was frustrated.

Neither of these situations has anything to do with research, teaching, or service. So, what is it? This is what I call politics. Trust me, you will find yourself in situations like this (and more) throughout your career regardless of how long you've been at this thing called professorship. You need to have some gamesmanship to maneuver these waters. No one ever teaches you how to navigate political situations like these and others.

Young professors are often very idealistic in their approach or their viewpoints. Or at least I was. With age and some gray hair (and a receding hairline), you will begin to learn that it is OK to lose the skirmishes so you can win the big battles. Sometimes, you lose those battles as well. How many times have you written a paper or a proposal, and reviews came back that you could hardly believe? How many times have you had to say, "I can't believe these reviews; this is ridiculous." You can insert any one of 100 reasons or phrases that you used here. You are idealistic in your approach. You only see your side of the equation. The best way to navigate politics is to begin to think about opposing viewpoints. It is often the case that, as a young professor, you may be blowing things out of proportion. Take the first example I cited. Is it really that bad that the young professor was not being selected to serve on important departmental committees? My advice to the young professor was to not get offended and continue to do what makes everyone take notice—doing good research, teaching well, and serving on relevant committees in the research field. Trust me. If you are successful in being recognized by national and international committees, then the department committee situation will work itself out. It is only a matter of time. Be collegial to the people you think are offending you and simply move on.

DEALING WITH JEALOUSY

For the second case, I provided similar advice to both him and a junior faculty member who felt that others in the department were jealous of him. Yes, some will be envious if you are successful in winning proposals and other awards and if you excel in your profession. You cannot control that. All you can do is be the best that you can possibly be. Be collegial and be aware of all situations. Ignore the ones who are jealous of you. When it makes sense, offer collaborative opportunities with the same ones who were trying to derail you. Enemies can become friends.

Years ago, a colleague of mine won three proposals in a row, and another faculty member in the department made some vicious remarks that the wins were due to personal favors. Yes, it is jealousy. My colleague took the high road and did not dignify the comment with a response at all. Don't lose valuable energy by responding to allegations.

Be careful with reactive emails. Emails are forever. When you feel like lashing out, do not sit down and type out and send a nasty email. Step away from your computer and take a break. After some thought, you will realize that it would have been foolish to lash out!

With this backdrop, here are a few pointers on how to navigate some (but certainly not all) political situations:

1. When you feel that you are in the middle of a sensitive situation, the first thing for you to do is to not react. You need to sensibly think about this and either respond or ignore. Take some time to think about it. Ask yourself if it is real or if it is your perception.
2. If the situation is real, then you must assess if it is worth navigating or ignoring. In some cases, ignoring things (such as jealousy) is the best solution.
3. In other cases, rather than seething on the inside, it is best to set up an appointment with the other faculty/staff member that you think is offending you and try to understand their viewpoint. Sometimes they are not really offending you; they are simply oblivious.
4. In all situations, never lose your cool. Be collegial.
5. I've had people come and scream in my office. I keep my voice level and repeat my point of view clearly. My blood pressure stays low, and I am able to keep my cool.
6. In every situation, you must discern what is going on. Wisdom is necessary.
7. Avoid shouting matches. They do no good.
8. Remember that learning how to resolve conflict as you move along in your career is excellent training.
9. Often, when it comes time for filling leadership positions in your organization, you are assessed for whether you are known for keeping your cool and resolving conflicts or if you are a poor manager of conflicts.
10. While the situation may be aggravating, use it as a learning situation. Learn well since this experience will help you navigate the next one.

Here are some parting thoughts: Probably one of the best things that happened to me early in my career was that I was purposely in incognito mode. Other than my fellow faculty members in the department, very few in the university knew me. A few years later when I had built up my research and teaching portfolios and reasonably established myself, I was able to venture into college and university committees. I called it the phased approach. I learned about the university culture and the "players" and was able to engage much better as an informed faculty citizen.

TAKE-HOME MESSAGE

As a young professor, learn how to focus on the three major items that you will be assessed by: teaching, service, and research. Blaze those trails. The rest will fall into place. Stay collegial and take the high road.

JOURNAL ENTRY

What are your own personal triggers when it comes to department politics? Are there active ways that you can emotionally detach yourself from a situation so you can see a broader picture? Do you have a colleague or mentor at a different institution or in a different field who can serve as a sounding board and give you honest feedback when it comes to political situations?

FOOD FOR THOUGHT

Think of a political situation you have been in and then identify things that you learned and think of alternate responses and potential outcomes.

NOTES

AN EASY TENURE DECISION AND YOUR DOSSIER

7

If you do not know this already, you will soon. The dossier is an evil monster invented by the bureaucracy of the university system to torture you, painfully, one year at a time. OK, that was an exaggeration. How about this one? The dossier is a document that you prepare, in exacting detail, when going up for either a promotion or tenure (or reappointment), and it is required by members of the university bureaucracy who love to waste your time. OK, only part of that was true. In most universities, the dossier is a ridiculously long document that contains (should contain) all the information about you

and your accomplishments. It is not enough to say that you are working on a $500,000 research grant. They want proof that the proposal was written, complete with the abstract and all the documentation associated with it. Yes, I can hear you clearly say, "You are kidding me. Aren't account numbers for each grant maintained by universities, making the account number the best way to identify grants in a dossier?" You are smart, but try telling that to the university system. You can tell how much I love the dossier system. Worse still, many universities force their faculty to enter all of the dossier information in a software program (there are many and these companies make a lot of money) with the "hope" that once it is entered everyone up the chain can easily access all that information. It probably works well in some universities, but it is never easy to enter all that information into a software system and expect great results.

I am going to make the assumption that you started your career at a university at an assistant professor level. This is early career at its best! The next step is promotion to the associate professor level. At this stage, most universities give you tenure, which means that they cannot let you go without due reason. Trust me when I say this—universities can be very clever about letting someone go regardless of tenure. Granted, this is difficult. But even as I write this section, I know that there are swirling debates about post-tenure review, doing away with tenure completely, etc. Regardless, you'll work your way to tenure. After all, it appears to be the holy grail in academia and a much-misunderstood concept by the general public.

In most universities, there is a yearly reappointment process for pre-tenure faculty that will (get this) put together a department committee to assess how well you are doing in (you guessed it) research, teaching, and service. Before you are awarded tenure, you *will* go through this process every year. Let me provide some guidance on how you should handle this.

Year 1 is relatively benign since you have just started. You will have to prepare a dossier and research statements, teach, and prove to everyone why you are worthy of reappointment for another year. You are probably scared because your dossier is pretty skimpy. It is reasonable for you to have a thin dossier during year 1 because you have just started your career. Your department forms a committee comprising several tenured faculty members from your department and at least one from your college. They read your dossier, deliberate, and write a report indicating that year 1 has finished and that you should continue to set course toward building a robust service, research, and teaching portfolio. Depending on the aggressiveness of your committee at the department level, they might suggest that you write a certain number of papers and teach relevant types of courses. They compose a long rambling letter and send it to your department chair. Your chair then conducts an independent review of your dossier and writes another report to your dean. Finally, your dean writes a report to the provost. By the time you get a letter from the dean, months have gone by since your reappointment process started. The letter from the dean is never going to be detailed because he or she is far removed from the day-to-day of your discipline. Therefore, it is important that you sit down with your department chair and ask for a complete debrief. Written comments are useful so you will know how to prepare for next year.

Your second-year reappointment process must be deliberate from your vantage point. You must take into account the first-year recommendations and then outline in your cover letter how you addressed the prior year's deficiencies (if any). Clearly indicate how you are succeeding in your goals for moving toward tenure. Do not wait until your review date to update your dossier. Update as you accomplish goals, teach classes, and serve.

This process (rigmarole) will continue every year for five years, typically. Each year you must build your portfolio carefully so that, during your year of mandatory tenure, there are no open questions from any of the committees on campus. At the end of five years, you will go up for tenure and promotion to associate professor. This is the mandatory year. If you are promoted and given tenure (or earned tenure as they would call it), then the biggest advantages are as follows:

1. It typically comes with a pay raise.
2. The university cannot let you go for flimsy reasons.
3. You do not have to go through the reappointment process ever again.

Having gone through it at many levels—as an assistant professor, as a committee member who had to write that dreaded letter, as a department chair who had to write one of those rambling letters, and now as dean—I consider it a necessary evil: a long drawn-out process and a lot of unnecessary work! So why do we do this? I'm glad that you asked. This is what keeps some lawyers in business. You'll hear this time and again. We need to make sure that we follow due process. Otherwise, we are liable to be sued. There you have it—straight from my two-plus decades' worth of experience. Having said all this, it is important for you to go through the hoops and come out with blazing colors at the end and with no scars.

First things first. You do need to know what the rules of engagement are. Read the dreaded faculty handbook on the criteria for promotion and tenure. Ask the department chair at the very beginning if there are departmental criteria and college criteria that you are responsible for. Get the criteria together and start piecing together your dossier. I suggest that you open up word-processing software and create subheadings. When you are really bored, start writing sections, one piece at a time. Make good use of some of those boring, large committee meetings. Look around the room. A lot of laptops or tablets are open. People are working through meetings and getting things done. (Someone is rolling their eyes and thinking that I am promoting bad habits by asking people to work during meetings. I'd tell that person to take one hard look in the mirror!) Moving on. . . .

I naturally suggest that you read through the guidelines and know the metrics. Doing so should be a nonfactor if you start looking at this from the university's perspective. However, I am not advocating that you put together a sloppy dossier. I strongly recommend that you look at rising stars in your department and ask them for their dossier. Hopefully, your department chair has some examples.

Ask your chair what's important for tenure. Pay close attention. Do something radical; email your dean and tell him/her that you'd like to either meet up or go out for lunch. Deans should be excited about this. I certainly am. Plus, the dean may pay for your lunch! At that meeting, ask what the metrics are, pay close attention, and come back to your desk and take notes.

Let's remove the mystery from reaching an easy tenure decision. Your entire dossier can be summarized into the executive summary that should—as I say—stand up and sing! The executive summary keeps the committee from having to look through the entire dossier.

MAINTAINING A DOSSIER

Let me tell you a story. A friend of mine at a university was a hotshot researcher, and other universities wanted to lure him away. Therefore, his university wanted him to go up for an early promotion so they could pay him more, keep him happy, and keep him from moving—you know the storyline. When he went up for his promotion, the chairman of his department was quite sloppy and failed to give him proper guidelines for creating a polished dossier. As a result, he prepared a very simple "dossier" that was nothing more than an extended curriculum vitae and sent it to the chair.

My friend prepared a CV that he thought would suffice as a dossier. He merely indicated the proposal grants and contracts, the papers and their full citations, and so on. The department fully approved this and the inept chair signed off on the paperwork with a hearty recommendation. Here's where the problem begins. The dossier and the associated paperwork went to the College of Science and were reviewed by professors (most of these professors sign up for such committees because they enjoy the process) from the other departments in the college. Scientists are supposed to be brilliant, but in this case, they rejected his application for promotion because (get this) the dossier was not prepared according to guidelines. Yes, the dossier matters.

Know this. Your dossier is evaluated first by your department. Everything after that stage is done by a committee that is looking at multiple dossiers. Therefore, reviewers always have a tendency to compare. Use that to your advantage.

Let's talk about how you can make your dossier shine.

SERVICE

Make sure you serve on committees at the department and the college level over your initial six-year period. It is not really necessary to serve at the university level. It is not a good idea to serve in the faculty senate since you are too new to the university system, and it is a time drain. There are too many committee meetings associated with the senate. I told you that I'd say it like it is at the beginning of the book, didn't I? It may seem that some of the committee meetings are a waste of your time, and you are right. There are definitely some time wasters! For example, the University Commencement Committee decides which rows the faculty has to be sitting in during commencement. On the other hand, some committees are indeed worthwhile, especially those related to student and faculty development. Figure out your time constraints and do not overcommit. If you are consistently serving on two committees each year at this level, you are doing well. Also, you should be serving in a reviewer capacity to journals and funding agencies; these fall under the service category as well. The service category should be easy to fulfill. As you move through the university, you will begin to serve and give more back to that university.

TEACHING

Course loads are wonderful things. Some universities have a 3 + 3 teaching load, which means three courses during fall and three during spring. If it is a 4 + 4 course load, I am surprised that you took that job in the first place, unless you have no interest in doing research. Teach well, empower your students to succeed, set expectations, and help students to meet those expectations. Create new and diverse courses that fit within the department framework. Keep student success in the forefront, and engage and excite them in the topic of interest. If you do, I cannot see how you can ever go wrong. Your courses can be tough and rigorous, but when you teach with passion, students will catch on. They will give you high marks and ratings, but that should not be your sole purpose for teaching. Integrate research into the courses, be available for students, and take ownership of the course. (If you have not caught on to my passion for teaching, something is wrong with my writing style.) Some say that you are doing well as long as the students are not beating down your department chair's door and complaining that you are a bad teacher. That is an absolutely negative way of looking at teaching. Teaching is not an intrusion on your research, and neither are students. This is an opportunity to empower the next generation of students. In six years, you should have taught a wide variety of courses, both undergraduate and graduate (if available), and developed some new courses as well. Some evaluators look for class sizes in the courses that you have taught. So be it! To me it is not about class sizes but about how passionate you are about teaching and helping students succeed. Do something outside the box. Ask a fellow faculty member (preferably a mentor) to come and sit in on one of your lectures. Ask them for feedback later. Better yet, ask your chair and dean (at separate instances) to come sit in on your lecture. Ask them for feedback!

RESEARCH

In six years, you should have accomplished quite a bit to make your dossier sing. You should have consistently published at least two to three papers in peer-reviewed journals each year, traveled and presented to one or two conferences, and lectured at another university. It is all about organization. You should have written multiple proposals so that you have won enough to support three to four graduate research assistants (GRAs) and should be well on your way to building a team. In fact, your research program should be so successful that you can buy your time out of teaching so that you are teaching one course per semester. All universities love this because you are generating revenue for the university, supporting GRAs, and helping with MS and PhD production. What administrator would not like that? If you get to this point in six years and place it in your executive summary, no one can argue with your success.

AWARDS

It is important to keep the "bean counters" happy. List the awards that you have received and show your upward mobility in the university and research community. If you take care of the research, teaching, and service portfolios diligently each year, then tenure is an easy decision. Think of it this way. If you always have a dossier and a CV (it should be up on your website) and it is of the high quality that is commensurate with rising stars in major universities, your current university will do whatever it takes to keep you there. Tenure, promotion, and leadership opportunities will follow.

JOURNAL ENTRY

Are you familiar with your university's committees? What committees do you think you would want to serve on and during what levels of your career? Why? Are there any that excite you?

FOOD FOR THOUGHT

If you have not maintained a dossier, make a plan for starting one. This may include looking at both stellar and abysmal examples. Engage with someone you trust so that you can get honest feedback as you work through the process of creating your dossier.

NOTES

TAKING CARE OF YOUR RESEARCH

8

In this section, I will make the assumption that your department expects you to conduct research and become a leader in your specialty of interest. Hopefully, you've already had a head start while you were in graduate school by writing student proposals and positioning yourself for a strong beginning. Or maybe you spent some time as a postdoc making yourself invaluable in your field by writing papers and doing top-notch research. If that is the case, then this chapter will provide some thoughts on how to maintain that momentum. If you are relatively new to the concept of building a research portfolio, then this is a good place to start.

You already have a PhD, so you know how to conduct research. I have never been a big proponent of writing a formal dissertation and then using

it to write peer-reviewed papers. In fact, I teach my students how to ditch a formal dissertation completely. They merely write papers, seam them together, and let the committee think that they have written a formal dissertation. Since it has already been vetted by peer reviewers in your area of interest, the committee merely gets to listen to you talk and watch while you sign documents— a mere formality. Here are some strong recommendations for taking care of your research.

YOUR DISSERTATION AS PEER-REVIEWED PAPERS

If you have not published your research, your first order of business is to make sure that you turn your research into journal papers as quickly as you can. The longer you wait, the harder it will become because you will have to start juggling teaching responsibilities. If you have already published your dissertation, then good for you! Sometimes my colleagues do not agree with the statement that the number of papers you write is as important as the quality of the papers. To be a prolific writer, you need to write several papers every year, in short and long formats. Writing in short and long formats is key since you cannot wait a year to write long papers only. The field may quickly go past your ideas, and you will miss your window of opportunity.

STAYING ON TOP OF YOUR FIELD

Whether you are young in your career or not, it is important to stay current in your field. This means you must read and assimilate papers quickly. This will continue to be your muscle. The more you read, the more ideas you will generate for research. The more ideas you generate, the more papers you can write. This means that you can write more proposals. Productive and prolific writing is a tremendous practice that will serve you well in the years to come. You will also be responsible for teaching your own students how to read papers, how to study and assimilate the material, and how to use it in their research.

Picture it. You interviewed well, you negotiated like a superstar (based on the principles in my first book, *Navigating Graduate School and Beyond*), and you have accepted the offer to become an assistant professor. You packed your bags, loaded everything in your car, and headed to a destination you'll call home for the next several years.

The first thing that you had to go through at your new university was new faculty orientation. You were forced into attending an arduous two-day orientation session at your university where administrators and university lawyers told you all the things that you were supposed to do (and not do). Even before you left the campus for the day, you had forgotten every bit of information on plagiarism, proposal preparation, etc. Welcome to your world! The next day you arrive at your department with grand notions of a huge window office with hundreds of square feet of space, executive desks, a printer, a state-of-the-art computer, and a personal staff assistant at your service, and you are greeted by the staff assistant who says, "Here's your office key." You open the door to what will be home—yes, home—for many more years and a still small voice in the back of your head says, "Did I make the correct decision?" Your office (if anything like my first one) has some used furniture that is assembled together to merely get by. But these days I hear that startup packages include generous allowances for fancy stand-up desks and state-of-the-art computers. If you were able to negotiate these items, more power to you!

Levity aside, you need to reconcile the fact that you are going to be busy and that there are huge expectations of you. Everyone wants to meet the newest faculty member! You have to quickly settle into your new surroundings. But take this piece of advice that I am about to give you seriously—very seriously. (In giving this piece of advice, I will make the assumption that research will be a major part of your portfolio at your university.) You must **carve out time** to stay current in your field and read journal papers on a regular basis!

In all the chaos, this is the first thing that early-career faculty neglect to do. Remember that you may be coming directly from a PhD or from a postdoc position where you continuously read papers to stay current. If you are good at research, you did not even realize reading papers was part of the core strength. If you neglect this aspect of your research focus, you will quickly become weak in your research. With that in mind, here are some guidelines:

1. Put together a set of seminal papers in your field, print them out, and place them in a conspicuous place in your office.

2. Print out journal papers on a regular basis. As much as I read using a tablet and a computer, there is a certain discipline in reading papers and marking them with a highlighter. It is also useful to note ideas in the margins of the papers for later reference. At another time, you can also pass the paper with the ideas to your graduate students and encourage them to follow a similar reading habit.

3. Do not read in your office regardless of whether you shut the door. Interruptions are always around the corner. Take the papers and find a place (library, coffee shop, etc.) away from the office, and then read and study the papers (no computers, no smartphones). Even if you read for a few hours a week in this fashion, you would be surprised how much you will progress.

4. If you travel to conferences, take some of those seminal papers with you as airplane reading to refresh your memory and create some new ideas.

5. Reading papers should generate new ideas constantly and motivate you to try to develop peer-reviewed paper submissions from these ideas.

As you move through your career, you will be asked to serve on proposal review committees for various agencies. This does not happen automatically, and simply asking to serve on proposal review committees may not be a good idea. If you write high-quality proposals, win proposals, and produce good peer-reviewed papers, program managers in these funding agencies will automatically solicit your help for reviewing proposals. Reviewing proposals is one of the best ways to keep up with the field because leading-edge ideas are being discussed within relevant literature. I hardly say no, even in this phase of my career, when it comes to serving in review panels for proposals. I make the time because it is important. I read many proposals and dig through the papers mentioned within the proposals so that I can catch and fill the holes that I have missed for whatever reason. Reading papers and keeping up with the research in your field should be an exhilarating aspect of your career. You must build a rigorous discipline!

IDENTIFYING PROPOSAL OPPORTUNITIES AS A TOP PRIORITY

You can have all the ideas in the world, but if no one funds you to do the work, then it is pointless. OK, I hear the Utopians sigh at that statement and say, "Research should be done regardless of funding." Hmm! Try writing that into the bottom line of the university budget. Better still, how do you think you are going to fund GRAs? There is no getting away from writing proposals. I'll review some basics of proposal writing at a later time, but you might be well served to read my first book where I go into great detail on proposal writing. The proposal submission office in your university probably sends out weekly or monthly bulletins regarding proposal opportunities. If you are relying on this bulletin, then you are being passive. As an energetic early-career faculty member, you should be doing your own work, setting up reminders to scour for proposal opportunities, and setting up automatic emails to receive notifications from various agencies.

AVOID BEING THE LONE RANGER

If you have not come to this conclusion already, then I hope I can nudge you along. It is difficult, if not impossible, to be successful in research if you are a lone ranger. It is important to network with colleagues across your department/university (if possible) and across the country and internationally. If you have data to share, look for someone who can use that data. If you are developing a product, think about collaborating with end users. In my line of research (satellite remote sensing), I am always looking to collaborate with people who are able to complement my research (experimentalists, numerical modelers, etc.). If you do good work and have a solid track record of publishing, people will readily collaborate. They can always read your papers (you have a website, correct?) and determine the quality of your papers. But be careful! Adding too many collaborators or promising too much and not delivering are bad ideas. Your collaborators will move on.

MAINTAINING A WEBSITE

OK. I am stating the obvious here. You really need to have a website. The goal of the website is to showcase your research, your team, and things that you are working on so that you are accessible for collaboration. Some have moved toward a blog format, but whatever method you use, you need to be able to quickly showcase your work to the university and the outside world. This is one way you can recruit students from all over the world and invite collaborative opportunities. I have received emails from Asia asking me to collaborate on a research paper because someone read information on my website. Insist that your graduate students maintain their own websites where they can discuss papers they are reading and research that they are conducting.

LEADING A VIBRANT, PRODUCTIVE TEAM

Often, I get asked to measure the vibrancy of a researcher or a team. I have a simple metric. At any given time, if the team is not working on a paper, reviewing papers, submitting revisions to papers, or working on proposal ideas and submissions, then vibrancy is questionable. Tall order, you say? Well, the vibrant teams that I know of are constantly producing high-quality research in various venues. Constant writing and publishing is something to strive for, and it will challenge your team. A vibrant team is an excited team that has papers being published, proposals being won, and conference papers being presented. Students are absolutely proud when they or their adviser wins awards or is asked to speak at major conferences. Bragging rights abound!

BEING A RESPONSIVE TEAM LEAD

I'll digress a bit here and talk about you as a team lead. With time, you will build a team consisting of students and researchers. Regardless of the number of people in your team, it is important to be responsive to member emails and create enthusiasm and excitement. After all, everyone likes to win proposals, have papers accepted, and win individual and team awards. It is your job to facilitate that and to lead the way. Therefore, as I have said repeatedly, never let a paper or a draft of a paper languish in e-space. Work with the student and get it out the door for peer review. Show up for meetings on time and make sure that your subject matter expertise is up-to-date. Students respect their adviser if they know that their adviser is a respected member of the research community, stays current in the field, and has numerous ideas. As a team lead, your ideas for research should far exceed the number of people in your group available to do the work.

TRAINING AND MENTORING YOUR STUDENTS

It is your responsibility to train your students to present their work effectively. Selecting and training students to work in your research group is critical for short- and long-term success. Good students will set the standard for the generations to come. Therefore, selecting and training students is critical. When selecting students for my group, I find that it may not be possible to meet with them face-to-face. All I have to go by is their academic record (GPA), their standardized test score (GRE), letters of recommendation, and their enthusiasm for research. I have had the honor of hiring students from many countries, and I have had the honor of learning from different cultures. It is an amazing responsibility to train and mentor these students. As an early-career faculty member, spend time looking through academic records, scores, and letters. These days, you can set up video calls with students and their advisers to get a sense of their communication skills. If computing and writing skills are important to your research, be mindful of those as well. Once you have selected students and they land on your doorstep, it is your responsibility to empower them to reach greater heights.

TAKE-HOME MESSAGE
Remember that taking care of your research requires active planning, time management, and inspiration. Your students look to what you are doing within your field and how you conduct your research to help plan their own futures. Being a team lead is both demanding and rewarding. Just as you are requiring literature reviews and productivity from your students, they are also looking to you to be the embodiment of leading-edge thought within the field.

JOURNAL ENTRY

How, exactly, is your research going? Have you found that you have fallen behind? What are some active steps that you can take to maintain your passion for your field? Think about a few of the team leads that you have worked under. Complete a strength, weakness, opportunity, and threat (SWOT) analysis of them. List characteristics that they had that you would like to build within yourself. Now, complete a SWOT analysis of yourself as both a team lead and a researcher. Where are you strong? What are the areas that you can improve? What are some steps that you can take today to improve?

FOOD FOR THOUGHT

Taking care of your research and being a brilliant team lead are not easy tasks. However, one thing to keep in mind is that no two team leads are the same. Remember that your team needs a leader who is solid enough to keep things in line and moving but flexible enough to see the needs of the team and adjust as the dynamics ebb and flow.

NOTES

BEST PRACTICES FOR PROPOSAL PREPARATION AND SUBMISSION

9

t does not matter what stage of your career you are in; whether you are an assistant or associate professor, it always helps to keep some guiding principles for proposal submission, especially when dealing with multiple people across campus. As an associate professor, you should already have a strong experience of working with the campus organizations that are responsible for submitting a proposal. Remember that you are not the person submitting a proposal to a funding agency. Whether you are submitting a proposal to NASA or NSF, your university is the submitting organization.

GUIDELINES AND POINTS
Time Management
Time management is key when submitting a proposal. It does not matter how successful you are at writing and winning proposals, you need to prepare the technical proposal in advance for your Office of Sponsored Programs (OSP) to review for compliance. After all, they are the ones who will hit the submit button. Therefore, be considerate of the process and timelines. There are some circumstances where you will be late turning in your proposal to OSP, but as long as it is not the norm, the office will probably be fine with it. It's unrealistic to expect OSP to do a top-notch job if you only give an hour for them to check your proposal for compliance and to submit.

Budgeting
The first item that I suggest that you do in the proposal preparation process—after you read the announcement, of course—is to take care of the budget. If you are the principal investigator (PI) with no co-investigators (co-Is), then the budget is a bit simpler. If the co-Is are from your department or university, have a discussion with them (face-to-face, please) and decide their role and contributions, which will decide their effort level (8% a year is 1 month per year). So that there are no miscommunications and misinterpretations, send them an email follow-up stating the roles you agreed on, the responsibilities, and effort levels, and ask them to raise any questions now. If you have co-Is from other organizations, then you have more work to do. Your university may be set up to help you with this process, or you may have to navigate this yourself. I usually talk with my co-Is, decide on the major factors, and then connect my OSP with theirs so they can get the templates ready. If you do not work on the budget in the beginning but wait until the last minute, you will have nothing but headaches. You need to send your budget manager the period of performance, the number of years, what the effort levels are, and all that you need to accomplish the tasks. Ask to review the budget and iterate with the budget manager until you are satisfied with the elements of the budget. Once it is done, make sure that other co-Is send in all the appropriate paperwork to your university's OSP. You can now call your budget "final."

Writing the Proposal
Once the budget is out of the way, you can work furiously on your proposal. Again, if multiple people are involved, you will have to start early to seam the pieces together. Never assume that the pieces that your co-Is are sending you can be directly placed into the proposal. It is your responsibility to ensure that your co-Is, in their haste of busyness, did not cut and paste from a student's thesis or other material that they do not have a copyright to. It does not matter which co-I sent you the material and if it is deemed as material that was

plagiarized; you as the PI are responsible. You cannot point fingers at a later stage. Another reason why you should give yourself ample time to review and check the written work! Many funding agencies run your proposal through software to check and see if plagiarism is involved.

Writing a proposal, if done properly, should be an exhilarating experience. You are pitching a new idea after weeks of hard work with up-to-date references and top-notch figures as expected results to a leading-edge program. Winning is wonderful, of course, but even if you were not selected for funding, the process itself should have been rewarding. Hopefully you learned a lot along the way, and it got you up-to-date on the literature in the field. If you do not win the proposal, I suggest that you write a journal paper out of the results. Make a convincing case the next time around.

USEFUL TIPS FOR PROPOSAL AWARDS

You have won your first proposal and you continued to write and diversify your topics, and now you find yourself in the enviable position of having multiple proposals funded with a small team of students and researchers that are helping you crank out even more papers and proposals. You are traveling the world, presenting at major conferences, soaking in the sights and sounds of Sydney, London, Bangalore, New York, and Fortaleza. But you still have to think about your budget. Some principal investigators have an innate knack for keeping up with budgets and being savvy. I had to learn this carefully.

Get a Monthly Balance Report

Make sure to get an end-of-month (EOM) balance report for each one of your grants/contracts. Read this carefully. It will tell you the name of the grant, the period of performance, and how much money was allocated in each category based on the original proposal. If there are discrepancies, sort this out early in the process. If you have a budget manager assigned to you to keep track of budgetary items, consider yourself fortunate. But even if you have a budget manager, it is good discipline for you to pay attention to these matters. After all, you wrote this proposal and won this award. Do not squander it due to poor management or, worse still, due to someone making a mistake in your university!

Track Spending

Keep a spreadsheet that tracks the spending in each award. I maintain a simple spreadsheet that tells me the name of the grants, the period of performance, and what the EOM balance is. I pay attention to who is charging to the account, and I compare the EOM balance for each award against the previous month to ensure that there are no serious discrepancies. Do this once a month.

At another time during the month, spend about half an hour studying your balances so that you will know that your team members will get paid and travel will happen (if needed) properly. Every category must be understood so that you know that the funds are being spent properly.

Meet with Budget Manager

Once every three months, set up an appointment with your budget manager to review your budgets and ask relevant questions. As the PI, you must know how to keep your research moving forward. It is your responsibility to ensure that there are adequate funds to carry out the project objectives.

Extending the Project

If a project is going to come to an end and if there are funds left over, you can request a no-cost extension (extending a project without requiring additional funds) from the funding agency. Make sure that the paperwork and approval process is done properly so that you do not lose money. Some agencies give you a no-cost extension once and sometimes twice. The reasons for a no-cost extension must always be of a technical nature.

As a PI it is your responsibility to mentor others in the group to become PIs in their own right so that they can move the team forward. Let me finish by saying that managing multiple projects is challenging but also rewarding because you get to carry out several research projects all at the same time while hiring students and other researchers to help propel your research forward. At the same time, this comes with the responsibility of keeping your team productive and motivated. If you are traveling too much and if your team does not get to interact with you regularly, there is bound to be lack of morale. Being a team lead and a PI is rewarding, but it has important responsibilities.

TAKE-HOME MESSAGE

Winning proposals is exciting, but it comes with accountability. As the PI, you are responsible for your team, including co-Is. Once you've gotten tenure, you have a reason to celebrate. So celebrate! However, there is still more ahead. Next comes the journey to full professor. Continue to expand your portfolios and take a special interest in the online revolution. Know the ropes of the proposal submission process to save you from stress in the long run, and remember to monitor your budget regularly.

JOURNAL ENTRY

Do you remember when you were the co-I and what it was like? Did your previous PIs prepare you well for the role? If not, what might you do differently to better prepare your co-Is?

FOOD FOR THOUGHT

Everyone likes to win. However, don't let not winning proposals discourage you from writing. Consider this: you'll never win if you never write.

NOTES

2

EMPOWERING YOUR STUDENT
+ BUILDING YOUR TEAM
= SUCCESSFUL RESEARCH

KNOW YOUR STRENGTHS, WEAKNESSES, OPPORTUNITIES, AND THREATS

10

This section is largely written with professorship in mind and for those who are interested in mentoring graduate students toward their PhD or Master's. No one ever teaches a course on How to Mentor a Graduate Student. At least, if there is one out there, I have not attended it. For most professors, their career paths looked something like this: Finish an undergraduate degree, struggle with a decision on whether to pursue a graduate degree, start a Master's degree, and then really grapple with whether to continue on toward a PhD. Eventually, when finished with it, they breathe a huge sigh of relief and then ask the question, "What now?" OK. Maybe that was a bit dramatic, but I am sure that several went down that path. After the PhD,

most ended up as postdoctoral candidates and some ended up as assistant professors ready to mentor and guide students toward graduate degrees. In most disciplines, very much like mine, the emphasis is largely on doing good research, taking courses, passing exams, and writing and defending their research. Rightfully so!

But where does one "learn" about mentoring students? If you had the privilege of being mentored by a good professor, chances are that you will emulate your mentor and follow that path. If not, what happens then? I hate to say this, but past experiences definitely shape the future. Take this case as an example. A professor I know was molded by an adviser who never relinquished control, let alone transferred ownership to the student. Even during the last stages of his research, the professor constantly checked the work of the student and did not *trust* the student. The student was bright but was constantly under surveillance. Needless to say, when the student became a professor and began to take on his own students, the lack of trust from his own graduate student days began to surface. He never learned how to train or mentor students, and this frustrated his students. Past experiences had shaped the future. This does not mean that all students who become professors will follow in the footsteps of their advisers, but it is second nature for the human mind to revert to what is familiar when there is nothing else to rely on.

This chapter is written for those who want a fresh start at mentoring students. For those of you who have read my previous book (of course, I strongly advise you purchasing it as I get a staggering $1 per copy), I make a distinction between advising and mentoring. Advising means that the professor is merely interested in helping students select courses, guiding them in their research, and ensuring that they finish their degrees. That far and no further! Mentors, on the other hand, will empower students to reach their maximum potential. They are interested in making sure that they help their students establish their careers and maintain healthy relationships even after they have graduated and flown the nest.

LEARNING YOU BEFORE MENTORING THEM

Let me set this up. Let's assume that you, as a professor, are interested in mentoring a student toward a degree and a successful career. I'll assume that you have already recruited and selected the student and you are ready to take on this huge task. Where do you start? Before you begin this exciting (sometimes frustrating) journey, remember that you need to know what your strengths are as a mentor. Never buy into the lie that either you have what it takes to be a good mentor or you don't. Becoming a mentor is a diligent process, not an innate quality or an event. Granted, you can learn from others' poor tips and advice, but ultimately you have to work at it yourself. Let me be upfront: most of this hinges on you developing a trusting relationship with your student. This is a common theme throughout this book. You must know your strengths and weaknesses as a mentor, opportunities that are available, and threats that you must overcome. In short, you must do a SWOT analysis on yourself.

Mentoring should be a key part of your portfolio, and it is set in the backdrop of your teaching, research, and service activities that you are already doing as part of your job. In my opinion, mentoring should be a required element for professors. Remember that you need to list these SWOTs as they pertain to you becoming a good mentor, not just toward securing tenure (although they are interrelated).

Strengths: You need to list your strengths as a mentor. Some of your strengths may be that you are a good researcher, communicator, and time and project manager. Listing strengths is easy, but sometimes what you think is a strength could be a glaringly annoying weakness. Therefore, you need to be open to review and criticism. Better still, you need to also have a mentor at this and almost every other stage in your career. Whatever it is, you need to make sure that you provide an honest list of these characteristics and ensure that you pass them on to your students.

Weakness: Everyone has some weaknesses unless, of course, you're perfect. In that case, I need to talk to you. Levity aside, list all of your weaknesses. Work on mitigating and, in some cases, eliminating them. The list of strengths that I've listed above could be weaknesses for others. For most struggling with mentoring, I've noticed that trusting the graduate student is a major hurdle. I'll talk about this more in further chapters. Other weaknesses include neglecting to set targets or voice expectations, lacking the ability to make the student experience success, not transferring ownership, being unresponsive or overresponsive, and being a poor listener.

Opportunities: You need to be aware of the various opportunities that can help you empower your students and inspire them to be better. Enable your students to secure travel scholarships and research fellowships. Always keep the students' careers in mind. Think about opportunities that you can provide that will enable them to build successful careers. While doing this, carefully explore opportunities that will enable you to become a better mentor. Look for formal or informal opportunities such as workshops (possibly provided by your organization).

Threats: You also need to be aware of threats that prevent you from becoming a good mentor. Are you a poor communicator? Then you need to overcome this hurdle so that your students know that this is achievable, even by professors! Whatever the threat is, learn how to mitigate it.

OK. Here is something I hear a lot. "I am too busy to become a good mentor. I cannot possibly do everything." All I can say is that you have to learn how to become a better manager of time to become a solid mentor.

WHY MENTOR A GRADUATE STUDENT?

This is a fundamental question, so I'll try to answer this in the most practical way possible. Here are some reasons (by no means exhaustive) for becoming a strong mentor to your students:

1. Mentoring a student should be, and indeed is, one of the most rewarding parts of being a professor or a faculty member. You were a graduate student once. Think back to that exciting time of learning new material and conducting research with someone who was an expert in the field. Now it's your turn! This is how the field grows.
2. You cannot solve all the research problems yourself. A graduate student, when properly trained and mentored, becomes a valuable asset and a member of your team. No, they are not cheap labor, as some are prone to label graduate students. They are valuable assets. Period.
3. Graduate students are inherently inquisitive. They have time to research an idea that you currently do not have time for. They can become valuable resource centers for your research.
4. They are your future colleagues and, sometimes, friends.
5. They are part of your legacy that you will leave behind after you retire and rest somewhere.
6. They are part of your team that you need to build to expand upon various research areas.

In summary, you need to provide for yourself a fair assessment of your SWOT so that you can work on these aspects.

TAKE-HOME MESSAGE

Before you can be a successful mentor, you need to know yourself honestly. Identify your SWOTs and make an effort to continuously better yourself. After all, your graduate students are a reflection of you.

JOURNAL ENTRY

I resolve to become the best mentor I can possibly be.

1. My strengths are _____.

2. My weaknesses are _____.

   I plan to mitigate these weaknesses by doing the following: _____

   _____.

3. My opportunities for becoming a good mentor are _____

   _____.

4. My threats are _____.

   I plan on reducing these threats by doing the following: _____

   _____.

FOOD FOR THOUGHT

Mentorship will be one of the greatest things you will do. Your ability to shape minds that will carry on your own research passions in one form or another will be what is left long after you are gone.

NOTES

BUILDING A TEAM

11

A young professor quickly gained success and won several grants in one to two years. As a result, he had to quickly hire postdocs and take on graduate students. Therefore, he went from being an almost one-man operation to managing a team of nearly seven to eight people in the first two years of becoming an assistant professor…except he did not realize he had a team to manage. He had not thought through the roles and responsibilities of the team members. Nor had anyone mentored him properly on effectively leading a team. Needless to say, this created considerable personal angst for him, and the team members resented his style of leadership (or lack thereof). Understandably, he began to lose team members.

At the onset, I need to explain why building a team is important—and fun. As a young professor, you enter into the world of the university establishment

with excitement and some apprehension. If you have not been jaded by the "glass half empty" kind of folks already, you are ready to take the world by storm through excellent research and outstanding teaching. Rightfully so. I wish someone had told me this during my first years as a professor—you can do more with and through a team than by using the lone professor approach.

THE FINANCIAL FACET

Research-intensive departments especially look at the bottom line. I am sure that you know this, but just to be sure, I'll say it anyway: the bottom line is money, pure and simple. Not just money that you win in grants and contracts but also how much of those dollars you spend on a regular basis. Let's say that you won a two-year $100,000 grant, and, just for the sake of an example, that total amount goes toward salaries (you and graduate students). When the budget was prepared, only $50,000 was for real salaries and the remaining was for overhead charges. The university draws from this overhead, or facilities and administration costs (F&A), when you charge salaries. This means that a bean counter somewhere is tabulating F&A generated by each faculty member for each month. The higher that number, then the higher the revenue your research generates for the university. While largely a bean counter perspective, it has its merits and problems. It's called F&A, but one of my colleagues explains it as a "tax." Guess how your light bill is paid and the salaries of those folks who walk around with a tie and suit all day. That was a bit harsh, but it's true. For research-heavy departments, you are known by how much F&A you created that year. You are a superstar if you generate the most money for your department and/or university. You are ahead of the curve and the favored one.

THE PRODUCTIVITY FACET

Given that backdrop, you have to quickly start thinking about what determines productivity. To get research funding, you need to make sure that you have leading-edge ideas. Hopefully you've read my first book and have already won proposals. It is not enough to have good ideas. You need people to work with you to solve the problems you have identified. Enter graduate students. By generating more ideas, you can write more peer-reviewed papers (of course, high-quality papers). By writing more peer-reviewed papers, you are seen as someone who knows how to complete projects and generate ideas. Your proposals are more polished because you are already using some of these papers to leverage them. I hope you get the point. For you to write more peer-reviewed papers in a wide swath of research areas and win competitive proposals, you need help. That's why you need a team. I know that some of you who are reading this book think that this is not that formulaic. I agree. If that were the case, I would have $500 million in grants and contracts. I don't. However, I've carefully assessed the success of several researchers and this seems to be the pattern.

Hopefully I have convinced you that you need a team, not just for productivity's sake but for the excitement of it all! I must mention the importance of building your team slowly but steadily. If you try to take on three graduate students and two postdoctoral candidates in the first two years of your career as an assistant professor, you are bound to get burned out. I know of a colleague who took on the responsibility of building a team too quickly, and the strain began to show in short order. He did not have the experience in managing time, let alone people. He was quite adept at research, but all of a sudden, he found himself dealing with human resource issues rather than research issues. He was late for appointments, forgot meetings, and lacked concentration during his meetings with students. Too much, too fast! Some of the human resource issues must be learned properly over time. Start with one student the first year, and add another student to the team only if you can handle both the tripartite (teaching, research, and service) and mentoring. I strongly discourage starting with postdocs the first year or two since that requires a different skill set.

THE LEADERSHIP FACET

I am often asked how a graduate student and team must be motivated. Here are some guidelines that I have found useful over the years. Each member of the team is different in many respects and brings various strengths (and obviously weaknesses) to the table. Therefore, it is your responsibility to understand those differences and work accordingly. Realizing these differences will go a long way toward promoting productivity. Part of promoting productivity is understanding that the team is looking for a leader, not a coordinator. That means that you have the responsibility of taking charge, setting goals, motivating, dealing with human resource issues, and communicating with transparency. While some tasks can be delegated to others, leadership responsibilities are yours and yours alone. You cannot take on recruiting responsibilities and then delegate termination responsibilities. Students want to be mentored by you, not your postdocs.

Part of being the team lead is setting the norms for the group. List them or talk about them at your group meetings. If attendance and PowerPoint presentations at group meetings are mandatory, then say so. If you expect Master's students to publish their thesis, then say so. If you will graduate PhD students only after they have published two peer-reviewed papers, then . . . you get the picture. Setting the standard is your responsibility. Whether it is excellence in the quality of research or the number of papers your group writes, you must vocalize this properly. In short, do not expect your team members to read your mind.

If you expect your team members to be responsive to your emails, you must be responsive to theirs. I've heard this story over and over. Adviser asks student to write a paper. Student receives no training/guidelines from adviser on writing said paper. Student sends adviser a draft of the paper. Student does not receive any input from adviser for eight weeks. This leads to a total loss of morale. There are numerous variations of the story that I just outlined. I have heard advisers tell me that the draft version of the paper was horrendous (but they never vocalized that sentiment appropriately to the student). I have also heard the student saying that there was no feedback. These are serious student–adviser mismatches that must be resolved through proper communication. It is crucial to provide solid training and good guidelines for paper writing. Tell your team members that they should expect to hear from you in a specific time frame and stick to it.

When I mentor young professors, I make it clear that it is absolutely imperative that they develop a "team culture" early on in their careers. They look at me quizzically, but it is rather simple. The team lead (you) must set the standard and stick to it. I am a stickler when it comes to the quality of figures in the papers that we write. I make sure that we have said everything in the figure the correct way (the size of the font, the color of the labels . . . I mean everything) before I am ready to release it for review. Some of this is non-negotiable while some allot for wiggle room. Some groups have norms and standards for the number of papers they publish or quality of a certain product they generate. Whatever the case may be, establish the standard and adhere to it. I've had the good fortune of having some excellent students at the beginning of my career as a professor. Once the quality of the papers (and the quantity) was established through these students, the others in the team and those who followed understood that the standards were high and the bar was significantly higher for team members. Fantastic, wouldn't you say? Team members set standards that were being followed by others that came after them. As the years have gone by, I've found that standards are never set on cruise control but require continuous work from me (as team lead) and others on the team.

The word "transparency" is all-encompassing and is often misunderstood. Team leaders must be transparent. While I consider it my strength, transparency is still a challenge. By far, the best thing that I can do is to create an excellent environment for the team to work in, listen to their ideas, and work alongside them to accomplish goals. An unresponsive or lazy team lead will not be able to maintain a long-lasting team. The team members simply get frustrated and move elsewhere. As a team lead, be transparent in your communication. If there is not going to be a pay raise a certain year, make sure the team knows that. It is better to communicate critical personnel items at team meetings rather than via email. Hiding behind email is a horrendous practice. Keep your eyes and ears open. Squash all rumors quickly. If a certain project will run out of funding, make sure the affected members know that well in advance. Instruct them in the rules of engagement. Involve team members in affairs related to recruitment. Their involvement in recruitment generates a sense of belonging.

It is important that you open up your home at least once a year so that the team will know you beyond your career. I often have a Thanksgiving or a Christmas meal at my home. Only one rule: no shoptalk. My team members have hung Christmas lights and stayed for nearly seven hours in our home getting to know my family members. When we have visiting speakers, I take my team out for dinner so that the team members can benefit from casual conversation outside the workplace. There are so many ways of making yourself transparent. There are several well-worn clichés such as "praise in public and chide in private" and so on. All that is true, but being a leader is more than that. As I've stated, it is being transparent.

Finally, let me get a pet peeve out of the way. However famous you are, you are not too big to stop what you are doing and talk to your graduate students/colleagues when they come to your office. I've seen (and been a victim of) several instances when a student is sitting in the adviser's office, and the adviser's body language says "I wish he'd leave." You owe your students undivided attention. If it means getting out of your desk and finding another chair to avoid distractions, then do it. Understand that it is rather rude to be typing or staring at a computer screen when your graduate student is conversing with you. I'm not asking you to have soft music in your office, wonderful personal pictures, and a conversation with an open palm to signify collaboration. At a basic minimum, face the student and don't type on the computer or be distracted on your smartphone (or whatever gizmo) while a student or another professional is trying to have a conversation with you.

As a final thought, building and maintaining a research team can be exciting and rewarding (and sometimes frustrating). Good things come to those who persevere. Building a team is a must for those of you who plan to write a lot of papers and engage in a wide array of research. Team building is also beneficial for career advancement. Often researchers with teams are offered leadership opportunities in academia, government, and other organizations.

TAKE-HOME MESSAGE

Research teams are great for producing ideas—and hopefully results! Ideas manifest as proposals and proposals manifest as funding, which leads to more teams, more ideas, and more funding. Remember to grow your team slowly. Be honest and upfront, and make sure to take the time to know your team outside of the work environment.

JOURNAL ENTRY

1. Talk to team leaders you respect and find out how they manage their team.

2. Write down your plans for building a team (number of researchers/students and approximate time frames for accomplishing your plans).

3. One of your team members has been missing team meetings of late. What will be your course of action?

4. Hire a graduate student to build a team web page highlighting your team's accomplishments and strengths.

FOOD FOR THOUGHT

How do you want your team to remember you? Think about what you need to do and what you need to avoid in order to make that happen.

NOTES

BUILDING TRUST

12

The following example of building trust is so profound that it is worth sharing. Years ago, a colleague of mine had trouble with one of his students. The student was not productive in her research. He concluded (with no proof) that the major reason for this lack of productivity was because she did not work enough hours. Therefore, he told the student that he would hold the keys to her office, and she should come to him each morning to obtain the keys. That way, he believed, he could track her hours. In response, all the student did was become more innovative in dodging her adviser. Bad strategy and a serious lack of trust.

Trust between the student and the adviser is a major component that propels the student to greater heights. Trust is easily broken and can be rather hard to build. For those of you who mentor students, I hope you know that it can take five years for them to graduate, sometimes more. Consequently, students are looking to you for advice and mentorship to help them graduate, land a job, and build their careers. All the while, you are also building your own career with research, teaching, and service. Pressure, anyone? That is why I believe it is important to start this five-year relationship on the right foot.

UNDERSTANDING EACH OTHER

For trust to work, both the student and the professor must understand each other. They not only must learn one another's strengths and weaknesses but must also learn how to walk in the other's shoes. When trust issues arise, they must learn how to ask the question, "What would I do if I were in her place?" Nothing is more humbling than walking in another's shoes for a while.

As a student, you must understand the stage of your professor's career that he is walking in. If these are early-career stages for the professor, this means that he is learning the ropes of mentoring. Hopefully you selected your adviser based on more than just how much the stipend was or the popularity of the university. If the professor is just starting out, there are bound to be some speed bumps in the adviser–student relationship. If the adviser is doing top-notch research and building (or has built) a history of peer-reviewed papers and grantsmanship, then just plan to work through these issues. Be mindful that minor issues should not be blown out of proportion. Recognize that your professor is working through various time-related pressures. He is constantly juggling research, teaching, and service duties. Be proactive in setting up appointments and work through research problems before going for help. Show the methods that you have tried rather than saying that something is not working. Become a resource center for your research that helps build your side of the trust relationship. Needless to say, maintain solid work ethics while you are a graduate student. I'll say this in simple terms. If you have solid work ethics and the fruits of your labor show in good grades and the higher quality (and number) of peer-reviewed papers, then your mentor will be happy.

As the professor, you should understand that there are also genuine pressures on your students. They are working through at least three courses every semester of their initial years of graduate school. They are learning new tools (programming, data collection methods, etc.) and getting the hang of research. Plus, they are also trying to figure you out—what makes you tick. At other stages of graduate school, they are passing qualifying exams and in many cases have families with real-world problems. If they are international students, there are a host of other issues as well: learning how to drive, live, communicate, and assimilate into a new culture. And do not forget being homesick! Therefore, trusting you could mean your fulfillment of the following responsibilities:

1. Keeping your word on appointments
2. Genuinely helping students through research
3. Providing the appropriate tools for them to work with (computers, equipment, etc.)
4. Giving them lead authorship when they have done and written most of the work
5. Trusting them when they have genuinely worked through a research problem
6. Building their careers by sending them to conferences and workshops
7. Challenging them to become leaders in their field
8. Making them assess their weaknesses and helping them to overcome them
9. Not using them for your own gains
10. Helping them communicate effectively
11. Nominating them for awards when appropriate

Lying to one another in a student–adviser relationship is the quickest way to break trust. If team productivity is the key (whether it is just adviser and one student OR several members), these principles are the same. Open communication is critical, and it is important that the professor communicates the norms and standards that are expected of the team members. It is equally important that the professor holds himself accountable to those standards.

PROFESSIONAL ETHICS FOR THE GRADUATE STUDENT

Probably one of the most difficult topics to tackle regarding graduate students is professional ethics. Why is that? We live in a world where there appears to be no one right way to do anything, so everything appears gray. You've probably heard the phrase "there is no black and white" or that when the situation is rather gray, the right thing to do is to leave it up to the individual. As catchy as that may appear, that type of thought process will land you in trouble when it comes to doing research or engaging in graduate student activities. While this section is largely geared toward professional ethics for a graduate student engaging in research, I will also touch upon some generalities. This list is not meant to be exhaustive, but it is pieced together from my years of experience as a student and an academic. I also have a unique vantage point as chair of a department.

Research

If your research involves data, the first thing to remember is to not alter, fudge, or change data. This is especially true if you own an instrument and make measurements. You have a professional responsibility to report the data as it was measured.

Reporting Results

It is imperative that you report your results with all of the methodology so that your results can be duplicated if necessary. This is definitely a professional responsibility because you have to allow others to learn from your research and build upon your work as well. For those of us who receive federal grants and contracts, it is important to remember that these research dollars were funded largely from taxpayers.

The same situation applies for the data that you collect that was funded by grants and contracts. It is your professional and ethical responsibility to make it available to everyone. Therefore, hoarding data for personal gains is not conducive to research.

We may all claim to be open-minded or broad-minded, and we may even have the highest degrees possible (a PhD), but we are all creatures of perception and preconceived ideas. When it comes to research, I have seen many researchers who desperately hope to fit the data to the preconceived conclusion. Bad idea.

Showing Data

When plotting results in figures from the data, it is critical to show all data, not just the figures that fit the best correlations. Often, it is in those outliers where some interesting research findings exist.

Plagiarism

Plagiarism is a difficult issue. I often tell this story to the students in my Professional Development course as a bit of an eye opener. When I was in the first semester of graduate school, I became friends with an international student who was also new to the program. As young GRAs, our job was to work on research topics with our advisers. Our advisers gave us state-of-the-art research papers to read and helped us through the process of doing leading-edge research. My friend's adviser was a no-nonsense, top-notch researcher in his mid to late career. He had a prolific publication record and was well known in his field. As students, we not only did research but also took courses to bolster our understanding and strengthen our foundation. In January of that year, just at the beginning of that semester, my friend's adviser gave him a journal paper that had just appeared in print. In my field, there are a lot of papers that appear on a weekly/monthly basis, and not everyone is aware of every paper as soon as it appears in print. As you go through this story, the key thing to remember is that my friend was an international student. My friend carefully read the paper that his adviser had given him and treated it like every other paper on his reading assignment in his class. This class was taught by a professor who encouraged his students to write project reports. My friend now made a huge mistake that he thought was not a major issue. He wrote a project paper for the course with several paragraphs and words taken from the paper that his adviser had given him. To make matters worse, the professor was excited about my friend's project paper and ideas, and upon reading the paper promptly walked to my friend's adviser and exclaimed, "Take a look at this amazing project paper!" You can already sense that trouble was just around the corner. My friend's adviser took a quick look at the project paper and not only proceeded to explain the problem but gave the professor the same copy of the paper that he had given my friend. Upon learning that the student had copied a lot of material from the paper, both the adviser and the professor were upset. The student was confronted and was quickly dismissed from the program on grounds of plagiarism. Some of you may feel that this was the right decision, and others may think that the decision to dismiss was rather harsh—especially since the student was not "aware" of plagiarism issues. It is, therefore, imperative that all students at the beginning of their research career, and at the beginning of every course, be reminded of plagiarism issues. It takes less than five minutes to do this, but it eliminates a lot of heartache for everyone involved.

Reviewing Papers

Often faculty (and therefore the students) are asked to review papers written by other researchers. Remember that when you accepted the responsibility to review this paper—I emphasize the word *responsibility*—you accepted the conditions set forth by the journal for reviewing this paper. An important clause is that you will not take the methods outlined in the paper and use it for your own gains. This means that you cannot reject the paper and then rearrange some of the ideas in that paper and publish it in another venue. This is certainly unethical. Granted, these things do manage to happen in real life. My advice is to practice professional ethics and stay aboveboard, and—guess what? —you can sleep well at night knowing that you have not stolen someone else's ideas. Whether you are reviewing a paper or proposal, it is important that you review it for its merits and move on.

Discussion and Debate

Here is a potentially explosive situation that was brought to my attention: "My wife's adviser did not allow her to publish her data because it went against the grain of his theories. He therefore delayed her graduation and frustrated her progress." What does one do in this case? As much as your adviser may be the world leader in his field, the first thing that you have to determine is whether the adviser asked the student to falsify the results. If that is the case, then I suggest that you find another adviser somewhere and distance yourself as far as possible from this person. No compromise. On the other hand, if you are only having disagreements in the way the analysis is being conducted or the methods that are being used, then make sure that you are not overamplifying the problem. Your adviser has more experience than you. Create an atmosphere for discussions and arguments that are productive.

Authorship

Another source of ethical conflict is the order of authorship on papers. Here is another story. A friend of mine, while in graduate school, was asked to write a paper to a major journal. His adviser let him believe that the student was going to be the first author. At the very last stage of submission, the adviser placed his name in front of the student's name. The student was upset, but the adviser indicated to the student that it was an executive decision on his part. As sobering as that story sounds, I have heard other instances of this lack of professionalism. Advisers should be in the habit of building a student's career, not frustrating them. Having said that, it is important to note that the rules of engagement regarding authorship should be outlined early on in the student–adviser relationship and reinforced at crucial junctures.

When collaborating with other scientists, most of the issues outlined above are still true. Establish rules of engagement upfront so that there are no misconceptions on authorships or responsibilities. Communicate effectively!

Professional Ethics

Professional ethics is a lot more than simply the examples and discussion points that I have presented. When confronted with ethical dilemmas, my recommendation is to carefully evaluate the situation before reacting to the situation. Apply common-sense principles and learn how to think about another's vantage point. If you are a student, think about your adviser's vantage point. If you are struggling with what you perceive as an ethical issue and you do not know what to do, seek out a mentor and work through the problem. Finally, most people that I know and work with are ethical and are genuinely interested in their profession. Therefore, do not make a mountain out of a molehill.

MANAGING YOUR STUDENTS

Does your student manage you, or do you manage the student? As part of full disclosure, you ought to know that I've already written a chapter in my previous book that is titled "Managing Your Adviser." It is probably the most popular topic by far when I travel and give talks or when I teach my Professional Development course. My premise for that chapter is that you, the adviser, are inherently busy (you should be or something is amiss); therefore, the student should learn how to take the reins of their graduate school work and become proactive.

Having said all of this, there is an element to managing your student. Keep in mind that each one is different. I've seen and have mentored students who have been independent, sensitive, lazy, prone to anger, soft-spoken, and loud-mouthed. I have had the student who manages time well and the student who shows up for exams late. I've seen a variety of students.

Know Your Students

It is important for you to know the strengths and weaknesses of your students. Write them down somewhere and see if your students' strengths and weaknesses are improving with time. Realize that not all students come with the same set of knowledge, skills, abilities, and work ethic; it is always a challenge. You need to spend more time with your entry-level graduate students as opposed to students who have been in your group for a while. Get to know the working rhythm of your students. If they have a series of midterm exams in a certain week, you need to expect fewer research results during that time period. Students take failure and disappointments hard, and you need to mentor them through some of these issues as well. Some students are not only balancing their research, courses, and themselves; they also have families, a spouse, children, and personal issues. You need to be aware of these situations. You're not there to be a close friend or a confidante for their personal situations, but it is part of your responsibility to be aware of issues that may prevent them from performing well.

Voice Your Expectations

I often sit down with my students at the beginning of their program and list my expectations. They include showing up for appointments on time, being responsive to emails, doing well in courses, being proactive, and maintaining trust. In fact, I tell them that they have to work hard at breaking this trust. All students enter with a 100% trusting relationship with me. If they break the trust (lying, fabricating results, etc.), then I will place appropriate measures for them to abide by. It works for most, but once in a while, a student will do something bizarre to break the trust even more, which then makes their life and mine difficult for a while!

Be Interested

As a mentor, be interested in their career paths. Ask them if they have a plan A and a plan B for their careers. Gauge their excitement and work ethic for achieving their goals. Then empower them to achieve their goals.

Teach Time Management

Talk about time drains. Encourage them to divide time appropriately between research, classes, and personal time. If you are not a good time manager yourself, send them to someone else for advice.

TAKE-HOME MESSAGE

Trust is a two-way street between the professor and the student. Work hard to maintain that trust as you manage your students. Unless students give you a reason not to, trust in their willingness and ability to do the work.

JOURNAL ENTRY

Do you find yourself wanting to micromanage your research team? Or maybe you're so trusting that you come across as uninterested because you rarely check in with your team? How can you find the balance in between?

FOOD FOR THOUGHT

Your students weren't chosen for you. You personally selected each one. Have faith in your decisions, and trust your students to carry out their deliverables on time and up to standard.

NOTES

TRAINING YOUR STUDENTS IN RESEARCH

13

I f I counted the number of times that I have been asked how to train students in research and my strategies, and if I were paid a dollar for each time I was asked, I'd be rich now. I probably would not be writing this book. I'd be on a tropical island somewhere. Just kidding! I'd still write this book.

Early-career faculty, whether they are just out of a PhD program or if they have just finished a postdoctoral stint somewhere, often think, "How bad can this be? I labored through research and watched my adviser go through this with me. All I have to do is get a good, hardworking, intelligent student and everything will work out just fine." Think again. Even though your adviser's tactics for training you in research may have been poor or marginal, your bad

experience—or lack of good experiences—should not be passed on to the next generation. With that premise, let's talk about some solid building blocks for training students in research.

If you have been diligent in writing and winning proposals and in ensuring that you have budgeted for a graduate research assistant, then pat yourself on the back. You've already accomplished something that early-career faculty struggle with. (I'll address selecting a good graduate student later in the book.) Now let's briefly distinguish between GRAs and GTAs. GRAs will take courses over the span of their degree programs and will work with you at least twenty hours per week on research problems. In a sense, they are giving you their undivided attention. On the other hand, GTAs are paid to help grade courses, teach lab sections, and often conduct research on top of that. They are also working on courses toward their degrees. That is indeed divided attention. Some professors argue that being a TA first is good because it is the rite of passage and it toughens students, etc. Be that as it may, attention is divided.

Now that you have a graduate student who is embarking on a research journey with you, it is important that you keep in mind some guiding principles. Needless to say, not all students are the same. Each student comes with a unique set of knowledge, skills, capabilities, and other traits. It is your responsibility to take these attributes and mentor the student toward a successful career. Early in my career, I made an assumption that when students walked through my door for the first time, I was supposed to talk with them and then give them a stack of journal papers to read. Bad move on my part! Some students relish the challenge while others get overwhelmed quickly. It is your responsibility as an adviser to develop this working relationship, not employ shock tactics. Some advisers still use such techniques today because they feel that this toughens students, and they falsely think intimidation is a good tactic. Try to reverse roles for a minute. You are 20-plus years old, you walk into an expert's office, and they scare you! Not conducive. Hope you are getting the big picture.

It's also important to realize that training a student in research is time dependent. I'll have to make the assumption that you went through a careful, deliberate process of identifying and selecting a student. Therefore, it is now your turn to start the research mentorship process. Graduate students who come to work with you on research may not be transitioning from your own undergraduate program. They need mentorship through six very distinct phases: Adjustment, Setting Expectations, the First Summer, Ownership, the Ramp-Up, Broadening Horizons, and the Celebration.

THE ADJUSTMENT PHASE

In the Adjustment Phase, you have to "get to know the student." Therefore, meetings must be frequent and not too far between. You have to take a genuine interest in the courses that they are taking. Talk to them about their classes. If they are struggling in some courses, relate your experiences and provide some tips on how to study. I often ask my students to go to the library and find an undergraduate version of the textbooks used in the graduate classes that they are taking. Building success stories for your students is critical. So is building their confidence. Give them a few research papers to read over that first semester. Teach them how to read and assimilate research papers. If you do this properly over the first few semesters, then you will build a strong foundation for years to come. Give the students some simple research problems as small, manageable, and confidence-building exercises. I usually give my students a standard satellite remote sensing primer that tells them where to get their first satellite image. I also give them a small piece of computer code to visualize the image. Experiencing small successes sets the stage for big ones later!

THE SETTING EXPECTATIONS PHASE

Now that the first semester has whizzed by, it is time to move on to the next phase of research work with your student: setting the expectations for the following semester and year. Tell them how many papers you want them to read every week and what types of papers. The whole goal is to train them to read journal papers and to build their research muscles. Ask the students to give a fifteen-minute presentation every other week on a paper that they have read. In the presentation, coach them on good presentation skills. If you have a team, let the students practice this talk before the whole team. Praise the students in public. If there are criticisms, save them for a one-on-one meeting. Constructive criticism is best. Building rather than tearing down should be your main goal.

THE FIRST SUMMER PHASE

I will assume that the Adjustment Phase and Setting Expectations Phase happened in the fall and spring semesters, respectively. It is now time for a summer dedicated to working research, especially in the student's *first* summer. This is a critical time when students typically do not take courses but concentrate solely on research. At least, that's what most of my students do. Students respond well when they experience success and when you set realistic goals for them. One of the goals among my team is to publish journal papers regularly, which are initiated by my graduate students and coached by their adviser (me). The summer goal is structured to support the academic year's expectations: gather the requisite data, analyze data, and develop a template for a journal paper to be published during the following year. I ask my students to come up with a title, list coauthors with the student's name first, set an anticipated submission date, write the chapter headings based on the journal that I have chosen, and fill in key pieces of the template. I have found that students are tremendously motivated when they see their names on draft versions of their papers. They are now ready for the Ownership Phase.

THE OWNERSHIP PHASE

The next fall semester has started, and with it comes more classes for your students and added teaching responsibilities for you. Now that you have been through a one-year cycle, it is time for you to start laying the foundation for the ownership phase. Students need to take ownership of their projects. It needs to be conveyed clearly that this is your goal. Students who take ownership go above and beyond what's asked or even imagined for that project. During the ownership phase, it is important for you to pose challenging research questions. Ask your students to think through those problems and get back to you in a reasonable time with answers. This is a critical stage since the research intensity is ramping up. You must work closely with the students to make sure that they are learning to connect the journal papers that they have read with the projects that they are working on. It is time to get that first paper completed.

THE RAMP-UP PHASE

Now that you have carefully worked with your students by building success stories, motivating them to high expectations, and taking ownership, you can now begin to ramp up the research productivity. Set the stage for more research and ask them to diligently work on multiple projects. All students like to experience success. Long, drawn-out projects with no or limited success wear them down. Purists argue that good work takes time, and I agree (partially). They also argue that it is better to write a definitive piece of work after many years as opposed to multiple compartmentalized pieces of work. There are merits to all of these arguments. I often help my students take their research and set it in a larger framework. Then I help them compartmentalize their work into multiple papers and challenge them to write several peer-reviewed papers. As they write more papers, they read more journal papers and learn to connect their work to other work in the field. This motivates them to be productive. Consider the alternative. Long, drawn-out, complex pieces of work that are never broken down into portions rarely motivate students. This is not about compromising quality or doing shoddy research. It is designed to publish regularly and help the student experience success regularly. Nothing excites my students more than seeing their work published with their names on the author list.

THE BROADENING HORIZONS PHASE

There are many areas where early-career faculty struggle when it comes to mentoring students. One particular area is trying to find a balance for their students between the courses that they have to take, various exams they have to pass to finish a PhD, and research they have to perform to fulfill the goals of the grant or contract. I faced the same pressures and challenges when I started my career and worked carefully to help my students find the balance they needed. You have to remember that you cannot separate student responsibilities into courses, exams, and research. It is important to guide them in a holistic sense since everything is interrelated like a Gordian knot. One complaint that I sometimes get from students is that the adviser constantly abrogates ownership of the tensions and challenges of the project and places them onto the student. That is rather unfair since your goal as adviser is to shield students from unhealthy tensions.

If students do not do well in their courses, they are not going to perform adequately in their research. It is important for you as the adviser to realize and communicate that the goal of taking graduate courses is to lay the foundation, and you need to help connect the research to this foundation. You must actively take an interest in selecting courses for your students. When they struggle with a course, find the appropriate resources to get them through it. I had a student who struggled in a core course; I shared a strategy that I used when I was a graduate student. If it is graduate-level material that they struggle with, then go to the library and find some entry-level books to help them study the material. Different authors have different ways of explaining the same material; this could greatly benefit the student.

When broadening the horizons, it is important that you as an adviser connect the links between the research that your students are doing and similar work that your colleagues are doing both around the country and the world. For example, a data-driven project could benefit from a simulation project, and making that connection is of immense importance to students as it helps them to broaden the horizon into the future. It is your responsibility as an adviser, not only to help them finish their current research, but to find an area of research that they can thrive in after they finish their graduate work. Again I say that it is your responsibility to make this happen. This keeps me on my toes since I have to constantly be on top of the literature in the field, stay connected with the researchers in the field, and have an appetite for publishing papers myself.

This next area is something that is easier said than done, and I am not hugely successful myself at this. Graduate students must be encouraged to take courses in leadership, human resource management, and business while they are in graduate school. I waited to take these courses many years after I graduated. In my current position, I can say without a shadow of a doubt that these courses that I took in the social sciences and in the business school are of immense help and should be a standard part of preparing students for their lives after graduate school.

THE CELEBRATION PHASE

If there is ever a party to throw for your student's success, find that occasion and celebrate it with enthusiasm. Student success takes many forms. They could present papers at major conferences, win awards for those presentations, publish papers, win fellowships.... The list is endless. When my students win awards of any kind, I make sure that I send an email to my group, mention them in my group meetings, and post that information on the board outside my office. When I became chair of the department, I did this for all students. I displayed a 10 × 10 poster in the department office with a picture of the student and a few words. The award information found its way onto the website. If it is a bigger award, now as dean, I make sure that it shows up on the front page of the university web page. Why do you think we all have different spheres of influence! Certainly it is for the collective good and not for individual accomplishments. I often sense the delight in my students when I make sure that I include them on a dinner outing. When I have a visitor for a seminar, I often arrange a dinner outing with all my students and the guest speaker. It helps the student see the social aspects of academic and professional life in a different context.

If I said it before, and I am not going to apologize for saying it again: It is imperative that you are always on the lookout for opportunities to nominate your students for awards. Trust me, there are many opportunities. Sadly, advisers are either lazy or too busy to take the time to write a page about their students and put together a nomination package for awards. Find these opportunities, make it the DNA of your group, and see your students win awards. It is pure gratification!

TAKE-HOME MESSAGE

If research is one of the core elements of your discipline, then make sure your graduate students are well versed in it. Semester by semester, train them up more and more until they're taking ownership of projects.

JOURNAL ENTRY

What journals might you employ for your student's first peer-reviewed paper? How is it different from a journal you would expect a veteran graduate to base their paper? Is there a difference?

FOOD FOR THOUGHT

Maintain that your students' success is your success. With that mentality, you'll want them to be their best and perform their best and be motivated to give them your best.

NOTES

GIVING UP OWNERSHIP

14

Whether minimalists or packrats, we all like to own things. There is something about achieving ownership that causes individuals to strive that much harder to reach goals. However, many graduate students go through graduate school never having experienced ownership of a project, let alone their own research. Let me explain what I mean a bit further. Professors are the ones who write proposals with ideas in mind. Proposals are often reviewed by panels of experts in the field. If a proposal is deemed worthy by the panel, then the proposal is funded and funds are given to conduct the research. There are many agencies that employ such a method. In the United States, the common ones are NASA, NSF, ONR, DOE, NIH, and other federal agencies. Private organizations also use a review mechanism that is very similar to a university approach.

When professors write such proposals, usually they request funds to support a graduate student. This is extremely important for young (and seasoned)

professors to do. It is sometimes tempting for professors to request postdoctoral researchers rather than graduate students since postdocs already have a PhD and their attention is focused completely on research. They are seen as being more productive from a research point of view. However, it is critical to realize, especially if you are in an academic institution, that training graduate students is critical. Yes, graduate students take courses and cannot focus entirely on research for the first couple years, but mentoring students is rewarding. After all, we were all graduate students at one time!

OK. I'll get off my rabbit trail and start my discussion on ownership.

The Role of the GRA

You've recruited a graduate student. You are excited for her to join the team and start on the research topic that you have designed. It is critical that the student and the professor understand the obligations. Remember that the student is being paid for this research assistantship: graduate research assistantships come with a decent monthly stipend, all tuition is taken care of, and often health insurance is provided. The contract for this indicates that the student work on research for twenty hours per week with the rest of the time spent on coursework. The student must understand that the purpose of the GRA is to fulfill the proposed research that the funding was provided for. This means that the student must deliver results so that, in turn, the professor can fulfill contractual obligations with the agency. Often, deliverables for such projects are peer-reviewed papers, conference presentations, or, in some cases, a product or an algorithm that has to be delivered by a set date. Therefore, the student must understand that there are consequences for not delivering high-quality (and -quantity) research as part of the project.

While this seems quite straightforward to some who are reading this material, it is not always clear to the student. I've written this down so that the professor can voice this clearly at the beginning of students' graduate careers. They need to know what's at stake. If this is established early on in the process, then it enables the student to celebrate the success of writing papers or delivering products. This sense of accomplishment goes a long way toward enhancing the productivity of the student. You should also explain the downside of not producing and not doing effective research. The student should understand that lack of personal productivity feeds up the chain and will therefore diminish future chances of funding, thus marginalizing the competitive edge of the team. I want to make something clear at this point. I've seen professors overdo the productivity part and browbeat students into "doing more." Not only is this counterproductive, but in my opinion, it is unethical. Constantly putting fear in the minds of students that their GRA depends upon productivity will only do more harm than good.

I am often asked how I strike a balance in all of this since some believe that I have a "knack" for training and mentoring—after all, one of my former students was an early-career Presidential Award winner. I do not have a knack or a magical formula. I tell some of the younger professors that all I do is provide an excellent environment for students to conduct research. This means providing top-notch computers, getting bureaucracy and paperwork out of students' ways, and having a genuine interest in *their* careers. The rest is up to the students. In return, I do expect the students to excel in this environment and be productive. I remind them that this is their career that is at stake—not mine. The students trust me, and I, in turn, do the same. I often tell my students that they start with 100% trust on the table. They are the ones who will reduce that trust by being unprofessional in their research and conduct. One of my colleagues indicated that he absolutely cannot tolerate students lying to him. I tend to agree. That will quickly diminish trust.

What Is Ownership?

What, then, is ownership? Remember that the professor was the one who wrote the proposal and, therefore, holds on to that research idea (now, a funded one) as a prized possession. The professor owns the research at that point. Rightfully so, since she came up with that idea and knows all the nuances of that research; therefore, she is the expert. The professor now has this fantastic opportunity to train and mentor a student in research. I've seen the next steps played in several ways. I'll describe two instances of professors choosing to retain ownership instead of transferring it to the student.

The first professor is a micromanager. This means that she knows what the final product should look like (or the paper) and she provides the student with small pieces of information. It could go something like this: "I want you to plot data A with data B and go through some analysis. Here are a few papers to read on this topic." The professor does not explain the big picture—or the forest (as an analogy). She merely talks to the student at the tree level (the piecemeal method). The student has no idea what's happening with the forest. He doesn't even know that they are in a forest. All he is told to do is to work through one tree to the next. The professor has total control and ownership of the project. I can understand this approach (maybe?) at the beginning of the student's career, but this is not a good method for students who are maturing in their research. Students will only go so far and no further if the professor keeps the ownership of the project.

The second example is of a professor who did not train his students in running a certain model. He was afraid that his students would make a mistake, so whenever those modeling simulations were required, he would run the model and provide results to the students. He did not trust his students and, therefore, would not give up ownership of the project.

I know some professors who are very adept at transferring ownership to the student and other professors who never do. In every case, the student who receives (and takes ownership) is always more successful. They become success-ful in the workplace while those who received improper training languish in their field. I am an optimist by nature, so I believe that if the professor transfers ownership properly, the student will take ownership and run with it. There are no questions of whether the student will take ownership when presented with it. I'll list some traits of ownership transference that you can use as signs that ownership has been given up by the professor and taken over by the student:

1. Students do not need to be constantly told what to do. Because students have a vested interest in the research, they are proactive in their pursuit of answers. As a consequence, they are often in their offices working out research problems and generating exciting results.
1. Students are excited to produce strong results that stem from pride that comes with ownership, rather than being pushed by constant probing from professors. Surprisingly, they want to—yes, want to—write peer-reviewed papers.
2. The professor begins to treat students like peers because of the responsibilities and personal investments the students have devoted to their work. For example, students often bring new literature that they have found during their research to the attention of their professors. By doing so, they are showing their commitment to staying abreast with the discourse in their fields.

All of these attributes are various ways that students take ownership not just of their research but of their fields of study.

HOW TO RELINQUISH OWNERSHIP

The trust relationship is working well, and the team is more productive. So, how does a professor give up ownership? Remember that you are not technically giving up anything; everything still belongs to the team. Rather, you are telling students, through proper training, that they have the responsibility to see the project through. I am sure that you will agree with me that the research field moved quickly between when you wrote the proposal and when you received funding. There are new methods in place and new data sets are available. Therefore, the student is best suited (with your guidance) to explore new ideas within the confines of the project. Here are some practical ways for transferring ownership:

1. Tell the students upfront that you want them to own the project. You want them to go from "our" project to "your" project. Let them know that with that come responsibilities.

2. Let them know that any new ideas that they generate within the project are theirs and the students will be first authors on papers. Build the students' careers. If you build theirs, yours will automatically be built.
3. Trust the students but expect them to make mistakes. Rather than hoarding all your data or models or whatever makes up your research, teach them how to conduct research. Challenge them to think about better methods to solve problems rather than the ones you proposed in your research. After all, you'll want your legacy to continue after you hang up your research. Correct?
4. When the time is right, take your students to a conference and introduce them to the major scientists and managers in your field. This signals to the students that you are serious about mentorship.
5. As the students mature, have them present at a conference or a workshop in place of you. Train them properly so the audience is genuinely impressed with both your students and your abilities.

These are only some suggestions. I am sure that as you keep in mind your students' careers, your ability to empower them will become more innovative.

TAKE-HOME MESSAGE
It can be easy to want to constantly look over your students' shoulders, but try to resist. You have to believe in their growth. Pay attention to their progress, and eventually you'll see when it's time to hand over ownership to them.

JOURNAL ENTRY
Would you classify giving up ownership as something that is difficult or something that is exciting? What milestones and traits will your students exhibit to let you know that it's time?

FOOD FOR THOUGHT
Your goal is to help put those three letters behind your graduate student's name. That will not happen if you never allow your students to own projects or challenge them to become their own resource centers.

NOTES

15

BE GENEROUS BUT GENUINE WITH PRAISE

A while ago, I gave a professional development talk at a major university. After I finished, there were two students who were trying to make eye contact. When the right moment appeared, they quickly walked up to me and, like secret service agents, whispered something like, "Can we talk with you later this afternoon?" I nodded yes, and I already sensed what the subject matter was going to be. This happens quite a bit after my talks. They came up later that afternoon, took me to a student lounge, shut the door, and then looked at me—waiting for . . . I do not know what. I am not a big fan of those silent moments, so I started talking about their research and the critical role they play in a team setting. What they did not know was that

I knew a lot about their adviser. Then they began spilling the beans. The silent ones at the beginning are always the ones that cannot stop talking.

The first student spoke up and posed this as a question: "What if my adviser is never happy with my research? What do I do then?" I listened and let the student continue: "I work hard and I think I am making good progress, but I simply never know. Every time I have a meeting with my adviser, he never tells me if I am on the right track or not and never tells me if I am doing a good job." (Did you catch that? The student wants affirmation!) He continued by saying, "In fact, I am not even sure that I am doing a good job. I wish he'd say something to that effect. The only thing that he ever says is that I need to be doing more or better or something like that. I do not remember him ever saying anything about my performance." Then I asked the student if his adviser has ever communicated what good research looks like. The student said, "I don't think I remember but I am pretty sure, no." I then asked the student if he had asked his adviser what good research looks like. He looked at me like I was from another planet, but he mumbled something to the effect of no.

There you have it. A classic adviser–student mismatch and, on top of that, a young adviser not knowing how to motivate with positive affirmation. Praise is important. You have heard that you must praise your team members in public and admonish in private. While that is absolutely true, students—especially students—can figure out quickly if your praise is sincere or merely a psychological trick. In my previous book, I asked the student to perform a SWOT analysis (strength, weakness, opportunity, and threat). I strongly suggest that you read that chapter, but here I'll work from the weakness angle alone. Since this book is written for the early-career professor, I want to focus on providing some practical advice since I often get calls or emails from young professors who are frustrated and who repeatedly ask the question, "How can I motivate my students?" I simply smile and walk them through some "Be patient" steps.

PRAISES FOR THE STUDENT

If you are an early-career professor, the demands on your time are immense. Add to that the pressure of wanting to succeed, wanting to get tenure, and, in many cases, wanting to start a family. It is difficult to place an estimate of age in this discussion, but let me say that you are thirtysomething and starting your career as an assistant professor where you are evaluated periodically on teaching, service, and research. All of that takes time. Most thirtysomethings that I know are married with kids (or wanting to have kids). Success at work spills over to all walks of life, and whether you like it or not, how you manage things on the home front spills over to the workplace. Constant dissatisfaction at home or at work is detrimental to the success of your career. Given this backdrop, you owe it to your students to provide a relatively stress-free workplace. This means that you have to think about the students and their careers and how you can empower them to become more productive. Therefore, it is important to understand your students, and it is your responsibility to take their weaknesses and turn them into strengths through their graduate careers. This means that you cannot have only your career in mind but theirs as well. With that in mind, here are some practical tips:

1. Learn your students' strengths and weakness, get to know their threats to being productive, and provide opportunities for success (and for praise!).
2. When they start the program, give them an overarching view of the project. It is OK if they do not understand it all, but at least they should understand your excitement and the magnitude of the project.
3. Break the project down into small pieces but help connect the dots in the early stages of their research.
4. At each opportunity, tell them what good research looks like and tell them if they've achieved it. By all means, be encouraging and offer praise. You may come from a culture where praise is not vocalized, but it is time to change all that!
5. With time, give them more independence and increased responsibilities.
6. At the start of the students' research, it is typical for them to handle only one project. But be mindful to not have them focus on one area too much at the beginning. You need to train them in a wide array of research, data, methods, and analysis techniques.
7. As students move through their research, give them other exciting projects to work on. Communicate deadlines. Continually challenge them to write papers. Remember my discussion earlier: If they give you a draft of a paper, turn it around quickly. Insert your comments and give it back to them. Provide quick, meaningful feedback and work rapidly through submitting a paper. One of my students still holds the record in the department that I currently am chair over—fourteen peer-reviewed papers in five years. He was a dedicated hard worker. All I had to do was provide the environment for excellence. He excelled!
8. Appropriate feedback and praise does wonderful things for students. They begin to develop a sense of purpose. Very quickly you can leave them alone; they are quickly becoming your peers. It is time for them to graduate.

OK. I don't have the benefits of only delivering praise. I've had tough decisions to make, and I have had to deliver some messages that students do not want to hear. If you have mentored to the best of your abilities and have been fair, and if things are still not working out, it is time to take some drastic measures: the firing of a student. Yes, I've had to let some students go for a variety of reasons. Oftentimes, we as professors make the mistake of holding onto an unproductive student for too long hoping that things will turn around and things will get better. Sometimes they do and sometimes they do not. I have numerous case studies of my own and from others and I will share a few here.

THE UNRESPONSIVE STUDENT

One of my former students was notorious for not responding to my emails and thought of the GRA as an entitlement. To make matters worse, I was on extended travel. He was not productive and always found the negative in research whether it was data or the method. In fact, he was not trying at all and not showing up to his office. In this case, all I had to do was have a heart-to-heart conversation indicating that if he did not shape up within three weeks, there was a long list of students who were ready to take his place on my team. I explained, once again, my responsibilities to the agency that provided funding for this research. (Sometimes you have to repeat these messages. I sense some professors nodding their heads!) I provided very strict guidelines on what he needed to deliver in three weeks and that I could not waste any more time. Within two weeks, he delivered the items I had requested and had turned over a new leaf. In this case, all was well—after a few months of agony. The next case was different.

This case was difficult, and I made some huge mistakes along the way. The student came from another country and was bent on doing his PhD. His grades were marginal (red flag!) and his GRE scores were average; I had no problem with either the grades or GRE scores. His recommendation letters were glowing, and someone that I had trusted gave rave reviews about the student. I was willing to overlook the grades, and I weighed the recommendation letter from the "trusted source" a bit more. The student appeared motivated, and the first semester got off to a reasonable start. I usually give my students the first semester to get settled in. I have very little in terms of research expectations except that they learn some tools and read and study peer-reviewed papers. I gave the student a very simple task with data sets that could be analyzed by using a spreadsheet program.

I always maintained an open-door policy for my students. If I am in my office, they can walk in and talk to me. This particular student never came to my office except for scheduled appointments. He would only respond selectively to my emails, and his habits were becoming a problem. This becomes a major issue for small- to mid-sized teams. Rather than focusing on productive research and teaching, precious time goes toward trouble management. At every meeting, the student began to show the same results, over and over, with no progress. On top of that, he was doing poorly in classes. All red flags. The second semester was drawing to an end, and I should have let the student go because, in spite of my repeated discussions and training, the student simply did not have the skills and abilities to complete a graduate program at that time. I convinced myself that it was a situation that could be turned around (while fully knowing that the skills and abilities were not a match). Rather than letting him go, I had now begun to draw stricter timelines and deadlines. The next phase of trouble had started. The student began to balk at the strict measures and began to accuse me of unfair treatment since he felt that others in the group received preferential treatment. Finally, after four long semesters, I had to let the student go. It was an unpleasant experience but a classic case of holding on to a student for too long.

In a perfect world, professors would recruit the appropriate students for their research based on knowledge, skills, abilities, and other traits (KSAT). In the real world, we get to know the students largely via email, applications, scores, and recommendation letters. Sometimes the match is not good enough. It is, therefore, imperative that you work hard at recruiting, training, and mentoring. If the signs to let go are there, it is time to make some hard decisions.

TAKE-HOME MESSAGE
Students need reassurance. Do not be shy about pointing out their progress and letting them know when they've done well. Conversely, know when it's time for more discipline and when it's time to let them go.

JOURNAL ENTRY

How many chances would you give a student before letting him or her go? In what ways might you try to intervene before it got to that point?

FOOD FOR THOUGHT

Everyone likes to know when they're doing a good job; otherwise it's easy to become doubtful or self-conscious, which can shine through in performance just as confidence and self-assurance shine through in performance.

NOTES

BUILDING SUCCESS STORIES

16

Your graduate student is a person with real emotions, feelings, and desires to succeed. She is in graduate school fully understanding what the opportunity costs (she could be making more money being in the marketplace). Often in the hectic pace of being a professor, teaching courses, doing research, traveling, and serving on various committees, the fact that your graduate student is looking to you for advice and mentorship is lost. If confession is good for the soul, then I will confess. I have sometimes struggled with placing mentorship on hold or putting it on the back burner for a while. When things get busy, oftentimes we begin to think that the students will understand if we place our time with them on hold. On the contrary, this can result in unfortunate consequences. Productivity

and morale can go down. If you have a team of students, word gets around quickly that you are too busy for mentorship. Therefore, be fully aware of your mentorship responsibilities.

With that backdrop, let me ask this question: Have you ever taken a graduate-level course where the professor only built the big picture and expected the student to work out all the details? If it is a semester system, this leads to three long months of agony and sometimes boredom for the student. Maybe it is a project-driven course, but everything hinges on you figuring things out and writing and presenting your work. I have taken courses like this and it was no fun. While some can handle this type of instruction and training, most cannot. They lose interest in the course and merely trudge through the mechanics to make a grade. Surprisingly, some professors employ the same method when guiding students in their research. They have one long talk at the beginning of the students' graduate careers and then provide some broad-brush research lingo laced with the occasional motivational speech, and they hope that students progress. Ever wonder why some of these students are not productive? Because they have not been mentored.

SUCCESS ON THE REGULAR

The crux of the matter is, quite simply, not all students are created equal, very much like not all professors and mentors are the same. Some students are independent and want to go at it on their own. I've had a few of those myself—although very few. Others come to graduate school to get a well-rounded experience. You are responsible for providing that experience as an adviser/mentor. If you are providing a graduate research assistantship for students, then you need to make doubly sure that you work with them on a regular basis. Most of my students have required training and diligent mentorship. My guess is that your students do as well.

With that in mind, I really want you to understand this: students require success stories on a regular basis. What do I mean by this? If students are working with you on research, then it is up to you to design research projects and themes that enable them to experience success on a regular basis. You cannot have a myopic view of the students' lives. Remember that graduate students take three, if not more, courses early on in their program. Plus, they are trying to balance research, you, a semblance of a personal life, and other issues. Think holistically! Therefore, design their research with specific success stories. Rather than only providing a big-picture view of the research (yes, there is a time and place for that), you should help the students break it down into doable, chewable chunks, especially early on in their research. Whether you like it or not, the generation of students that we are working with is different from the ones I have heard about or what I used to be. They are visual, want quick feedback and appraisal, and are sometimes impatient for the final product. Some of them are quick learners and have an uncanny desire to make their research meaningful to the larger community. Hope you caught that—they want quick feedback. Not necessarily instant gratification, but relevance is important to them. This is the Facebook and Twitter era. Quick and meaningful results at regular intervals are needed. So, if you operate on the premise that "all good research takes time—lots of time," then you are setting yourself up for some student–adviser mismatch. Read on!

COMPONENTS FOR STUDENT SUCCESS

How do we provide success stories for our students? Know your students, maintain regular contact, and determine how often you should develop these success stories. If they are good at programming and are still learning the content of other material, build the first set of success stories around their programming abilities. If the reverse is true and they are still learning their way around programming but have good analytical skills, build the first set of success stories around these analytical skills. Let me draw an example from my hands-on graduate-level Satellite Remote Sensing course that I teach. Satellite remote sensing is the science of using data from satellites for various purposes. My course focuses on the earth–atmosphere system. During the very first lecture (eighty minutes long), I make sure that I teach them absolute basic programming (in IDL) and write out a piece of code (about ten lines long) that the student can use. I ask them to try it out before the next class. Over the years, I have received various comments that indicate that they were initially apprehensive about a hands-on course in satellite remote sensing, but the fact that they were able to quickly display and see an image (a work of their own hands translates to a success story) provided them confidence. Granted, the entire course is not all that easy, but providing periodic success stories encourages the students rather than losing them to disillusionment.

In the initial stages of research, it is critical to build a balance between designing success stories and challenging the students. Therefore, mentoring through spending time together is important. Set specific tasks on a biweekly basis that students can then work through. Ask them to bring results to you. Encourage, correct, and challenge them to achieve the goals that you have set for them. As they progress, encourage the students to attend a student conference and write and present a paper in a major conference. Perhaps the biggest success story that you can build for your students is to help them write a peer-reviewed paper. Nothing excites students more than seeing a peer-reviewed paper with their names on it, especially as first author.

GUIDELINES FOR CREATING SUCCESS STORIES

Explain the Big Picture

Explain the big picture view of the research being conducted and how it fits in with the work going on in the field. It is the adviser's responsibility to paint the picture of the larger context of the research. Expecting the student to understand the broader picture in the first stages of graduate school is impractical and fraught with danger. I have heard advisers say this is the responsibility of all graduate students. Wrong! Paint the picture, leave out a few spots if need be, help the student color various aspects, fill in details, take away things, add things, make mistakes, and walk through the process with your students. It is an amazing journey for both of you.

Break Down the Big-Picture View into Smaller Chunks

Swallowing large pieces of research at any given time is painful. While maintaining the big picture, help students break down research into smaller chunks. Help them write papers in these smaller chunks. Let students present their work in bite-sized pieces and ask them to build this into the big picture. Often, I draw the analogy of research as a huge puzzle. The individual pieces must fit carefully to create a whole.

Design Success Stories Appropriate to the Graduate Student Timeline

As stated, success stories are important, especially for a graduate student who is in it for the long haul. Just writing and doing research, analyzing data, or building projects could become tiring. Why not send your students to a conference? Better yet, take your students to a conference, introduce them to your colleagues, and help them get and stay motivated.

Meet Regularly to Assess Success Stories and Motivate

Meeting regularly with your students is critical. It does not matter how busy you are. It keeps both of you accountable. Nothing breaks trust quicker than when you suddenly stop meeting with your students and then two months later walk into their office and demand outrageous results. You simply have not been involved in the research affairs of the students.

Design Research Papers for Student and Major Conferences

Use research conferences to put together targeted research projects so that students can write and present their work in a focused way. Short-term conference papers can be used to develop a longer-term journal paper. I use this approach for students who have trouble completing projects by deadlines. Conferences dictate a deadline; therefore, the students and you must hold to this deadline. Conferences require whoever is presenting to submit an abstract or a paper based on their presentation prior to the conference date. If the presenter (meaning your student) doesn't submit in time, there will be no presentation. And remember, quality counts!

Design Research Papers for Peer-Reviewed Journals

It is your responsibility to mentor your students through the process of writing their papers. They will especially need your mentoring through the first few papers as they learn the ropes and find their feet. I've heard students say that their adviser expects them to write papers, but they do not know how or even where to start. It is your responsibility to explain the entire process from start to finish. If you need help writing papers yourself, check out my first book. They need to know how to set up an outline, which journal to submit to, how to format, how to write, how to structure the paper, how many figures to use, and much more. Once you do this job well the first few times, they will latch on to the process quickly. Never let a student wander aimlessly trying to figure out the process of writing a paper; they need to be concerned about the technical matters discussed in the paper.

TAKE-HOME MESSAGE
Students can become impatient and disillusioned. Allow your students to experience success by first breaking larger projects into smaller ones. Help them to see the bigger picture and why each step matters.

JOURNAL ENTRY

How can you break larger projects into smaller projects? At what stage do you begin increasing the size of the portioned-off projects?

FOOD FOR THOUGHT

Remember back to the days of primary school when you'd take a math class and find yourself asking, "When am I ever going to need this?" Make sure your graduate students understand their roles and how each piece ties into the larger scope of the research.

NOTES

17

SETTING THE STANDARD

am often asked by early (and not so early) career scientists about how standards should be set for research groups. Great question. By "standards," I mean high-quality work that will lead to recognition not only in the department and university but also across the country and around the world. It all starts with you as the team lead. Team leads that have high standards (not unrealistic) are easy to spot. They have a set of core standards that they are not willing to compromise when it comes to research quality. Here are some strategies for setting these high standards.

HAVE CLEAR RULES FOR WRITING

When selecting journal papers to publish, high-standard team leads are not drawn to magazines to artificially raise their profiles. Neither will they publish

in journals that have low standards and high acceptance rates. Reputable team leads seek out journals of high quality that are read by a wide audience and will move their field forward. When writing papers, they have high standards for the literature review. They provide an in-depth and broad literature review without a lot of self-citations. When developing methodologies, these team leads do not purposely hide information so that others cannot follow or trace their work within field discourse. Their results and analysis are well thought out and are executed with high rigor. The figures and tables are of exceptional quality. Even when papers come back that indicate major revisions, they tirelessly persevere to publish in the same journals with solidly developed rebuttals and work that improves and elevates their papers.

If you are beginning to form your group or you have a large research group, it is important that you verbalize these standards often and ensure that your group members stick to them. Teaching students not to cut corners in research is critical. It is only through engagement with your team that you will develop the ability to spot any shortcuts your students may be taking; it is a crafted skill that is honed and developed over time. It is your responsibility to address your students quickly and effectively. My students, for example, write a lot of computer code to solve problems. No matter how easy it is for my senior students to share code with new members of my research team, sharing code like this is strictly forbidden in my group. In fact, it is a rule in my research group that code must be checked by me before it is shared. While it seems harsh at first glance, I am trying to help my incoming students develop their strengths from the ground up. No shortcuts.

We also have another rule in my group. All papers must go through my desk for edits and approval. Students cannot submit papers on their own. This practice ensures quality and a discipline that is enduring. Furthermore, my students cannot contact researchers in the field to "pick their brains" on issues. Students must figure things out on their own, and I am always there to help. Policies and standards like these help students develop at the correct pace and finish their research on time. More importantly, it prepares them for the workplace.

VOICE EXPECTATIONS

Unvoiced expectations are meaningless. Take this example. A faculty member is known for always whining about his students to me. "They cannot write well these days! They are not conducting data analyses properly. Their figures lack rigor. Their literature survey is abysmal. I used to do this so differently when I was a student. . . ." Are you getting the picture? I finally sat down with this faculty member and asked the question, "When was the last time you told your student about your expectations?" I was met with silence, and then he blurted out this answer: "They are supposed to know!" Herein lies the problem. Unvoiced expectations by an adviser will leave students frustrated and eventually will lead to loss of motivation and morale. I encourage early-career faculty members to clearly voice their expectations, not all at once, but over time. Paint a complete picture.

If students are starting their graduate work with you, train them on how to effectively read papers, take notes and annotate, and review material. Teach them how to trace the conversation the papers are a part of. Are there researchers or scholars engaged in a "discussion" that would benefit your students by observing the mechanics of their debates? This is part of teaching them how to actively read and understand journal papers. Set the standard, ask questions, make them stand up in front of a whiteboard and write down their thoughts regarding that paper or a series of papers engaged in a discussion.

Later on, voice your expectation about the quality of figures. Show them what is important and what your standard is. Go through a few papers and tell your students that this is the quality you expect. Concrete examples help. Show them lower-quality papers and tell them that those types of figures are not acceptable. The same approach applies to methods and analysis. Set the standards, train them, and mentor them. You will realize that your students will catch on quickly and become independent. The worst thing that could happen to you, as an adviser, is that your students struggle during the last semester before graduation with something as simple as making appropriate figures and tables. Training your students in various facets of research is your responsibility as an adviser.

SCORE GOALS

There is a lot of information out there, including books and videos, about setting goals and moving toward their completion. Goal setting in graduate school is very important. Let me give you an example from my graduate school days. My research was going well, and I was sure that I was going to complete it within the set timelines. But then I started hitting snags and began to regress. I found myself traversing rabbit trails. For those of you who think that rabbit trails are part of research, I agree, but only to a degree. I have known students who enjoy the scraps of lettuce on rabbit trails so much that they forget that their original paths had large patches of carrots. It is too easy to either enjoy the trails too much or get disillusioned with them. Either way, get off those rabbit trails and get back on the path of success and completion. Where was I? See, it is way too easy to get off on a rabbit trail! To help pull myself from those trails, I finally decided to print the first page of my dissertation. It was the title page, and I put a date of completion and stuck it right above my computer. Every day when I walked into my office and sat down, it reminded me that I needed to finish my dissertation. That was my motivator. The elation when I finished included the physical act of walking into my office and ripping that piece of paper to shreds. I was finished with my dissertation! As an adviser, it is important for you to motivate students to set goals and accomplish them. Do not forget to celebrate important milestones along the way.

Setting goals for your own career is very important. Realize that if you have resolved to be an academic for a while that this move is a long run akin to a marathon. Run too fast and you will burn out. Run too slow and you will be left behind. As I have mentioned several times in this book, you need a mentor to help you calibrate to the system. When I ask early-career faculty what their first goals are, it is no surprise when they say tenure is one of them. I hate to be the bearer of bad news, but this is a really bad goal. In the not too distant future, tenure may be a thing of the past. So setting your goals on tenure alone is problematic. Set your goals in terms of courses you'd like to teach, students you help succeed, number of papers you want to write, number of students you want to mentor, and meaningful committees you want to make an impact on. Set standards for yourself, develop a set of core values to go with them, and watch yourself succeed to high levels.

PREPARE YOUR STUDENT FOR THE QUALIFYING EXAM

A while ago, a student walked into my office after having failed the written portion of the qualifying exam. In most programs, a qualifying exam is a necessary hurdle in moving toward a PhD. The programs that I have been associated with have a written portion. If the written portion of the hurdle is cleared, then the oral portion of the exam begins. Remember that it is the committee (a team of usually three to five) that writes and grades these exams. The committee for the student that I mentioned above had five members. The exam is usually over two days, in this case nearly seventy hours—yes, that includes eating and sleeping, although I know that most students hardly sleep. This exam tests the PhD proposal that the student has written, and the committee members (CMs) test the student on some difficult issues related to the proposal. Everyone knows that this exam is challenging. In most programs, a student is considered a PhD candidate *only* after the student clears this exam. If each CM writes two questions, then these ten questions must be answered in seventy hours. It's a tall order, but these are the guidelines that are put forth by the faculty members in the department. Enter stress!

Written Exam

The first thing that the student must do for the written portion of the exam is to prepare a solid proposal by carefully outlining the methods and the expected outcomes. I recommend reading my first book on how to write a proposal. After the student writes this proposal, the committee and the student meet to go over preliminary details and then the questions are written. Mistake #1 for the student is looming around the corner. The student doesn't make contact with the CMs before or after they write the questions. Mistake #1 for you, the adviser, is also around the corner. You never told the student to consult the CMs.

With these two mistakes, a big disaster is about to happen. The student reads the questions but doesn't have an understanding of the expectations of these questions. If the question is broad or vague, what are the expectations? Does the student know? What is the CM expecting? This now becomes a mystery. Remember that the student has seventy hours and each question must be passed at a grade or a level set forth by the department. This communication mismatch comes up quite a bit. It is equally frustrating for the student and for the adviser who heads up this committee. Even capable students who are qualified to pass this exam panic when confronted with ten questions in seventy hours. With the expectation that they cannot communicate to anyone regarding these questions, another serious mistake is about to happen. Google search. Rather than thinking through the questions carefully based on what they already know, the student begins to search the internet, books, and any other material that they can access. Then at the very end of the seventy-hour mark, there is a huge rush to put all the answers down quickly. At this point, all the student has done is show their skills at searching for material rather than showing the thought process behind their answers.

Several issues are at stake here, and in the busyness of the day-to-day world, a communication breakdown has occurred. As an adviser, your first responsibility is to train and educate the student on the expectation of the questions. It is your responsibility to do the following:

1. Clearly outline the expectations of the written exam and make sure that the student understands what the CMs expect for answers—the breadth and depth of the exam.
2. Ask the student to communicate with the CMs regularly, especially before or after they have written the questions (of course before the student takes the written exam).
3. Go through some specific examples with the student on how they should be answering the questions. This is why you need a whiteboard in your office to sketch these issues down. This is mentoring at its best.

Failing an exam is disappointing to say the least. In the case of this student, I heard the gamut from "How can I expect to answer all these questions in seventy hours?" to "Are there even answers for these questions?" to, more interestingly, "I did not know what was expected of me." The student was defensive, teary-eyed, upset, and frustrated.

Much of this could have been prevented with some open discussions at the very beginning. I did not feel the need to read the student the riot act and send him out of my office, but I clearly explained that the exam was not a searching exercise but an attempt to figure out what exactly the student knew regarding the subject matter. Not what has been written elsewhere, but the analytic thinking of the student.

Now the next big-ticket item is up next: the oral exam!

Oral Exam

The oral exam would have been a disaster for this particular student since he was not well prepared. What does the oral exam entail? Oftentimes the CMs (in this case five members) will ask the student various questions regarding the research proposal. In most cases, the questions will lead down the path of how well the student can connect the principles learned in the courses to the research proposal in question. This is where you as the adviser can play a major role in preparing the student for this exam.

Note that not all students have the same level of maturity and diligence in planning for an exam of this magnitude. And also note that the oral exam is quite intimidating—five PhDs "grilling" a student on what they know or what they expect the student to know. Here are some practical guidelines for you as an adviser:

1. Three to six months before the oral exam, you should spend at least one hour every week with your student. In this session, you should ask the student to use the whiteboard in your office and go through these sessions as though they were the actual oral exam. Note that when you first start, students are apprehensive and do not know how much to write on the board or what to write. It is your responsibility to methodically train the student.

2. It is the adviser's responsibility to train the student to take research ideas and outline and then map out the essential tools. You should indicate the top ten items that the student should master and clearly explain using the whiteboard. These are the essential tools of the qualifying exam. These may be concepts, equations, or other paradigms that the student must have complete mastery of. Why is this important? If (most probably when) the student panics or freezes during the actual oral exam, you as an adviser can gently suggest that the student explain one of the essential tools that they have mastered (relevant to the question that is being asked) to the CMs. When confidence is built in an oral exam, the student will do well. This type of preparation is key for the student and must not be taken lightly.

3. Clearly set the standard for your student and make sure that she understands the expectations of the CMs at this level.

4. Every week the student should make progress. At the end of the three- or six-month period, if the student has not made progress, then they are not ready to take the written OR the oral exam. Never set your student up for failure.

5. Make sure that the student reads the appropriate material in preparation for the exam. Most students have a good idea of what to read, but it is up to you to mentor them on how to prepare and what to expect.

Hopefully these tips will help you realize both as a student and an adviser that passing these exams based on a research proposal requires more than an equal partnership between the student and the adviser. If anything, it requires more from the adviser to make sure the student is adequately prepared and informed. I have been asked several times as to how should one specifically prepare. Here are some really great tips for you to pass along to your students:

1. Remember that when all else fails, you need the ability to go back to the fundamental concepts. In my discipline, atmospheric science, I ask the student to read/study/memorize (just kidding) the entire book by Wallace and Hobbs (*Atmospheric Science: An Introductory Survey*) very carefully. This has the building blocks of most atmospheric science topics from dynamics to cloud physics, radiative transfer, and general circulation. If you get stuck in the oral exam, back up, present the fundamentals, and work your way from there. If a student can do that well, I will vote for a pass.

2. Know your stuff. If we as CMs ask you the top five research papers in your specific field of interest and you have no idea how to answer the question, you are in trouble. Knowing papers, the key authors, and their work in specific detail is part of the preparation process.

3. This exam will very clearly reveal whether you have been reading/ studying key journal papers. Remember that this is an exam that is for PhD candidacy. Knowing your material at this level is critical.

4. Take at least six solid months to prepare for an exam of this magnitude. Lay out a plan, assemble the key books, notes, and papers, and take good notes.

All of this is to really build your own confidence. If you are confident in the exam based on the preparation it will show and passing this exam should be easy! The student, after all, is a reflection of your mentorship. Empower them to succeed in the qualifying exam.

TAKE-HOME MESSAGE

Set the standard for your research team and communicate it thoroughly. Don't compromise. Show your students exactly what you expect from them to help prevent misunderstandings.

JOURNAL ENTRY

Telling your team what you expect from them does not make you a dictator. As the professor, you are both captain and coach. Explain in detail the rewards that are often a result of your standards and the consequences that may ensue for any shortcuts.

FOOD FOR THOUGHT

The qualifying exam is nothing short of a big deal. Although the exam consists of the students answering the questions, teaching your students to ask the right questions can help them to better prepare.

NOTES

MEETING WITH YOUR STUDENTS

18

I f you are a superstar researcher and if you do not have time for regular meetings with your students, this section is not for you. For those starting out as professors and who have or want to mentor students, this section is useful.

ONE-ON-ONE MEETINGS

Students greatly benefit from regular one-on-one meetings with their advisers/ mentors. I suggest a weekly meeting—unless of course you have thirty graduate students, but I know very few with that many. Weekly meetings usually should last an hour, with time allocated for various aspects. Remember, I am talking

about students who are working on research topics leading to their thesis/ dissertation. Weekly meetings are a time to catch up on the students' lives in general, find out how classes are going for them, and discover how research is coming along. I often break down the research discussion into subcomponents.

1. **Reading Journal Papers:** Students should be challenged and held responsible for reading and studying journal papers. At the beginning of their students' graduate careers, mentors should provide an array of papers for their students to study and read. Some seminal papers should be studied, and others should be read and relevant points noted. A portion of the weekly meetings should be used to test the student on the papers that they have read for the week or selected concepts/components of the paper. Students should be encouraged to become resource centers for the topics they are working on. Refer to my previous book on becoming a resource center.

2. **Building a Foundation:** Depending upon the discipline, build core strength that includes courses necessary to understand and conduct research. This is usually straightforward, and most academic programs have this outlined in the departmental catalog. Encourage your students to avoid shortsightedness by taking only the minimum number of courses for graduation. They should take as many courses as possible to build a well-rounded background.

3. **Acquiring Tools:** This is a critical part of the students' program of study. Programming skills are critical these days, not just for research but also for future jobs. The students should take programming courses or courses that are programming intensive to acquire these tools.

4. **Using the Tools:** With the foundation that has been acquired, perform research based on guidelines of the project.

5. **Communication Results:** Use presentations and peer-reviewed papers to discuss project results. The more papers that a student reads, the better off they will be to place their results in the context of what they have been reading.

6. Repeat steps 1 to 5.

WEEKLY MEETING
1. Check to see how courses are going for students. Make sure that they are taking the correct courses to build foundations and tools.

2. Spend about twenty minutes on the agreed-upon paper that the student is there to talk to you about. Ask the student to use the whiteboard to explain concepts. (If you do not have a whiteboard in your

office, talk to your department chair and make sure that you get one. This is a top priority.) Explaining concepts is a confidence-building exercise for your student. As they move through graduate school, many of their exams will involve a committee who will require them to explain concepts on a board. By starting the student on a whiteboard on a regular basis, much of the fear about standing in front of people can be minimized. Make sure that the student does not merely repeat what the paper has said. Make them dig deep to explain concepts. If they cannot explain the important concepts, ask them to reread. Provide pointers. Explain some of these concepts yourself and leave room for the student to go back to his office to think and figure out the rest of the problem. This is an extremely critical part of the training. Use this time wisely. Do not browbeat the student, but make sure that he knows what you expect from him. This way he will be better prepared for the next meeting.

3. After this, you should ask students to show you what they have been working on in their research. What tools have they been using to solve problems? What figures or plots have they generated? What analysis have they conducted? This is where the "rubber meets the road" aspect of your meeting commences. You should let the students explain what they have learned. It is tempting to jump in and explain all aspects of the figure or analysis they are conducting. Resist this urge. Teach them how to analyze results—after all, you have the experience. As they mature, you will be able to see their confidence growing. If they are not maturing from one year to another, most of the blame should be with the adviser. Unless, of course, the student has not put in the time required for research.

4. The last five to ten minutes of the meeting should be a genuine attempt to get to know the student. Some of my students are from other countries and face immense challenges. This should be a time to address some of these issues.

Note that scheduled one-on-one meetings are not the only venue for getting to know students. When I was a student, I enjoyed impromptu appearances by my adviser to shoot the breeze. I make it a point to do this even now, not because I have to, but because I enjoy these times with my team. I learn a lot from my students—research and otherwise.

GROUP MEETINGS

I know that some professors resort to group meetings because their groups are large or they do not have the time for regular one-on-one meetings. I do not recommend group meetings for those of you who are starting your careers. For those who have a team consisting of students, postdocs, and other staff, it is definitely beneficial to have regular group meetings in addition to the one-on-one meetings with graduate students. Graduate students are special. They should receive focused attention from their mentors. In the group meetings, it is important that the team understands the progress that is being made on all projects.

I conduct weekly meetings (one hour) for my team of about ten to twelve people. Everyone gets the floor for about five minutes. Students prepare PowerPoint presentations before the meeting. Individual members of the team get to showcase their research in three or four slides only. I asked them to discuss an itemized list of the work from the previous week, one to two key figures that can be explained clearly to the entire audience, and plans for what will be accomplished the upcoming week. As a team lead, I too prepare my PowerPoint presentation so the team can see my research activities.

If your team is larger, you may need more time or you may think about having sub-group meetings. Each month, I ask a member of the team to present results from a recent paper of interest or an overview of a paper that he or she has written. The PowerPoint slides serve two purposes for me:

1. They provide accountability as a record of everyone's progress.
2. They serve as a reference when I write reports, which is more productive than sifting through email updates from multiple students.

TAKE-HOME MESSAGE

One-on-one meetings allow you and your student a chance to get to know one another. It's also an opportunity for students to build up their research skills, communication skills, and presentation skills.

JOURNAL ENTRY

You're busy. Your students are busy. How can you make sure that you make time for meetings? Are you for or against using technology if meeting in person is next to impossible?

FOOD FOR THOUGHT

Making the time to meet with your students shows how invested you are. Every week may not always be possible, but it is ideal. Missing an occasional meeting isn't a spirit breaker, but don't make a habit of missing too many.

NOTES

3

LIFE AFTER TENURE: WHAT TO EXPECT FROM ASSOCIATE TO FULL PROFESSORSHIP

19

SWITCHING GEARS

The tenure year came. You took all the advice that I've given you seriously, so of course you were granted tenure and a promotion. You have garnered a pay raise and probably some stability—at least in your mind. I hope this does not mean that you will stop thinking about moving to higher levels of excellence (if so, that means you can stop reading this book here and now). But before you go, let me assure you that there's a lot more fun to have beyond tenure.

WHAT'S NEXT?

First things first! Celebrate your success of achieving tenure and promotion to associate professor with friends, family, and colleagues. Savor the moment

because more work is on its way. Make sure that you update your web page and signature blocks in your email with your new title. Not all places in your university will automatically change your title from assistant professor to associate professor in brochures and web pages. Contact the appropriate people and make sure that the changes are properly made.

Recently, I had a conversation with a colleague of mine who was promoted to associate professor with tenure, and then year after year went by—six years to be precise—and nothing was happening in his move toward full professorship. When I asked him why, he startled me with this answer: "When I came to this university, everyone talked about tenure and no one discussed life after tenure." Some of you reading this could say, "Well, you should know better" or "That is your responsibility." But leaving aside that argument for a minute, it is imperative that we have a mentoring system in place that guides faculty toward full professorship and beyond. Not all faculty members who have received tenure and promotion to associate professor know what to do next in terms of achieving full professor status. Do they do the same types of things that they did to achieve tenure or do they adjust strategy? Who do they turn to with questions? Some departments have excellent mentoring programs and workshops for associate professors. Other places simply let you fend for yourself.

If you've set your goals early on in the process for *only* obtaining tenure, then major adjustments are needed. However, if you have put together a comprehensive view of your career and academic path, then only minor adjustments are called for. First things first though. Take another trip to that dreaded faculty handbook and take a look at "Promotion to full professor." It might say something like this: *A professor must have the terminal degree in a pertinent discipline, except where the individual has achieved equivalent status through outstanding performance. A professor also must have attained authoritative knowledge and reputation in a recognized field of research or creative achievements and must have maintained high levels of effectiveness in teaching and in service.*

Notice how cleverly these things are worded: "authoritative knowledge and reputation," "creative achievements." If you are a scientist, you are thinking this right about now: "How does one measure this?" This is the major reason why some universities end up in legal battles over words. It certainly keeps the lawyers employed! It is often difficult to quantify these metrics; therefore, it is up to you to ask questions, write them down, and deliberately develop a plan toward achieving those goals.

Regardless of the long-term goals you originally set out for yourself, it is rather straightforward when making the decision to promote to full professor. It is up to you to take care of business. It is important to switch gears a bit after tenure. If you are one of those who must know how long it takes to get to full professorship, then by all means do some quick research and figure out how many years it took faculty members in your own department to move from associate professor to full professor. Myths probably abound in most places that it will take fifteen years to become a full professor. Hogwash! Unless there are some rigid rules in universities (I doubt it!) regarding the number of years that must pass after earning tenure, you can start preparing for promotion as early on as associate professor. Trust me though, there is probably a dean or another administrator somewhere who is bent on looking at the total number of professors, associate professors, and assistant professors in balance in a department, as though that means something!

TEACHING PORTFOLIO FOR THE ASSOCIATE PROFESSOR

How, then, does one become a full professor? You must remember that being a tenured member of the department means added responsibilities and duties. Yes, you guessed right. You can now participate (!) in all of those committees reserved solely for tenured members. The goal of becoming a full professor is, in my book, rather clear. You should not be benchmarking with anyone in your department, college, or university. You need to be thinking about having a CV that is good enough for some other university to come knocking on your door. I am not asking you to leave your current university. But having options helps you gain a larger perspective.

Let's talk about teaching courses for a minute. You taught several courses that involved large and small class sections during your pursuit of tenure. You probably taught graduate and undergraduate courses. Maybe your department even allowed you to develop your own graduate-level courses. This is all well and good. But you need to think about flexing your teaching skills a bit when preparing your journey toward full professorship. Like it or not, it is up to you to make sure that when you submit your dossier for promotion to full professor the various committees on campus from the department, college, and university levels have no foothold to complain. Let's assume that you are planning to apply for full professorship six to seven years after you were promoted to associate professor. Some may say that it is an aggressive schedule. But remember that your CV and, in this case, your dossier are going to do the talking. It is important to start thinking about the success of your students in a more methodical way. Come up with some ideas to enhance students' successes in your courses. Your dean and provost are going to adore you now (not that you should do this just to impress someone in the hierarchy). But you now have some breathing room. I am quite sure that your university is hungry to increase student success, retention, and time to graduation (graduation rates).

If you are teaching undergraduate courses as part of your portfolio, think about developing some new formats for teaching your courses.

Traditional Courses

While you may have been trained in the classic style of a whiteboard with Power-Point slides, newer methods are beginning to emerge everywhere. Many universities are thinking about using collaborative techniques or experiential learning methods to enhance student participation, success, and engagement. You may have heard fellow faculty lament about how attention spans are ridiculously low in the current generation and how they expect rapid feedback for even the slightest item on the syllabus. Whether you like it or not or believe in small attention spans, it is still your responsibility to teach effectively. Some of your classes may be well suited for students to do collaborative learning to solve problems. Even though I graduated ages ago, I still remember a top-notch hands-on assignment where one of my professors in a graduate-level class used a simple but effective way to convey the concepts regarding the urban heat island effect. For those of you who are not familiar with this concept, it can be simply described as the changes in temperature due to urbanization. The professor split us into teams and gave us thermometers to measure temperature at every block through urban and rural areas (at which point it was not a block anymore). We collaborated with the various teams, and we presented as a group the changes in temperature. I still remember the concepts from that project vividly. However, I now have to think about the legal forms that these students would have to sign for a project like this, which alone could be an arduous process. Regardless, there are ways to get students, even in a calculus course, to work with one another. Yes, I hear you say that collaborative learning in class is nothing more than doing homework in class instead of going home to do the work. I get that side of the argument as well. But if you get started on new techniques that get students working together, then maybe—just maybe—they will begin to connect outside of class!

I would strongly suggest that as an associate professor you attend at least one teaching conference per year to learn about some of the new ideas that are helping students succeed and engage with the course material. Better yet, after an appropriate amount of time, volunteer to give a college-wide or even a campus-wide seminar on your journey from teaching using conventional methods to other, newer methods for helping students engage better (yes, I am making the assumption that it is better). While you are helping the students, you are getting outside your comfort zone, gaining tremendous insight, and enjoying the experience. You are also letting your university know that you are a productive, engaged teacher with the best interest of students in mind. You are becoming indispensable! You can also clearly state in your dossier that you have reached high levels of excellence in teaching.

Online Courses

The craze (or is it craziness!) to get more university courses online will only continue to increase. There are raging debates in the community on which is better for the students: an online format or the brick-and-mortar methods where the students engage with the instructor in a classroom. The writing is on the wall if you look at the number of high schools that are beginning to have online courses. Students like the convenience of taking courses at their own pace and in their own environment. In a revenue-hungry model, why wouldn't universities rev up online opportunities? What's my take then? I bet you want to know. Here's a diplomatic answer: Some courses may be better suited than others for online learning, but we need to make sure that the quality of the online curriculum is high. If your university wants you to simply run a voice over PowerPoint slides, then run away from it! If there are instructional designers who will help transform your content into material that is online-worthy, then that is the way to go. Regardless of what I think, get ready for the online revolution. It is already here and it's about to get even more interesting. If you are not in the business of creating knowledge through discovery and then applying it to courses, then you are going to have a hard time finding or keeping a job!

Now that I got that out of the way, let me also say that you may be in an environment where online learning is done correctly. There is a strategic plan in place for online learning. Appropriate resources are being allocated. Incentive plans are being designed for instructors. Students are learning the material and moving through their degrees properly. This will be an environment where you as the subject-matter expert can make great contributions to the online selection of courses. Universities with shoestring budgets cannot pull off a good online structure or a selection of courses. Without resourcing this properly, it is doomed to fail. Regardless which environment you find yourself in, think about taking one or two of your courses online to reach a larger audience. Of course when it is successful your university will not share all of that revenue with you, but at least you can expect a thank-you!

Specialized Courses

Finally, talk to your chair about developing some new specialized courses that dovetail your research. In graduate-level settings, these are the types of courses that equip students with the knowledge to land good jobs. Not only will the employers thank you, but the research community is in need of such qualified students.

The goal for your teaching portfolio is the same as always: have a diversified portfolio, help students succeed, and engage students effectively. But remember that very few, and I mean very few, get to become internationally known for their teaching effectiveness and methods. Therefore, research is where most of the efforts are placed for promotion to full professor.

TAKE-HOME MESSAGE

Once you've gotten tenure, you have a reason to celebrate. So celebrate! However, there is still more ahead. Next comes the journey to full professor. Continue to expand your portfolios, and take a special interest in the online revolution.

JOURNAL ENTRY

What motivates you to want to pursue full professorship rather than stopping at tenure? What steps should you take to reach that goal?

FOOD FOR THOUGHT

Ponder this: Would you rather the promotion to becoming a full professor be an established number of years, or is it better for the professors to set the pace for themselves?

NOTES

RESEARCH PORTFOLIO FOR THE ASSOCIATE PROFESSOR

20

For teaching-intensive departments, most dossiers going up for promotion will look similar and include a record of courses taught, student evaluations, ideas about new teaching methods, and even some teaching workshops attended. For research-intensive departments, you are not going to impress many with a teaching-intensive dossier. That's simply the way things stack up. I'm going to make the assumption that your department and college are research-intensive. This means that the expectations are rather demanding, quite standard, and very business minded. What is going to set your research portfolio a cut above the rest?

PROPOSAL WRITING

Allow me to reiterate: your ability to write and win multiple proposals is absolutely key. Whether you like it or not, this is what is going to make your CV

marketable. You should be writing multiple proposals with the purpose of supporting GRAs, adding a percentage to your salary, and supporting postdoctoral researchers on your grants or contracts. If you are doing this, you have certainly hit the sweet spot in research. Most universities will not tell you this, but I will. Every time you win grants and spend them, you are generating overhead (tax or facilities/administrators costs), and there are several administrators in your university who track this amount each month. Yes, each month. I hear you say, "That's ridiculous! You make a university sound like a business and much less like a place of higher learning." You got that right! Universities look at bottom lines, much like any another institution. You can whine all you want that a university is not a business and should not be run like one. Have you looked at the salaries of your administrators—especially the president and vice presidents? After you've taken a look at that, maybe you'll come to the realization that these are large businesses. Why do you think one part of the university clamors for increasing enrollment while another for increasing research funding and another for raising funds? I hope it is sinking in! If you are in the top echelons of bringing in research grants and contracts consistently over several years, it is harder for anyone to deny you a promotion to full professor. This does not give you the license to become arrogant or myopic in your thinking that the world revolves around you. I've had "superstars" sit across my desk and tell me why they are worth every dollar of their salaries and read me their accomplishments. They even tell me that they are not happy and insinuate that they will leave the university if things do not change. I do not subscribe to superstar arrogance; you have to be good at what you do with humility and class. Superstars come and go, but team players stay to become leaders and serve an organization well in the long run!

Let me provide a small tip for proposal writing at this point. I strongly recommend that you take a look at my previous book, which details how to write effective proposals. As an associate professor you have to remember to enhance your portfolio of proposals to increase your chances of winning proposals. What do I mean by this? Never give up your bread-and-butter research ideas and venues when writing proposals. If you have had a track record of writing and winning proposals in certain subject areas, then by all means continue to do so. This is what is supporting your graduate students and postdoctoral researchers and part of your salary as well. It took you a long time to develop these ideas, establish a network, and be known for such work. Don't give up your position as a leader in this area. While you keep your bread-and-butter ideas churning, you need to diversify your research interests to slowly start venturing into other research areas as well. The best way to do this is to collaborate. If you are a laboratory scientist, you may want to collaborate with a numerical modeler. If your work is making field observations, maybe you can work with a statistician. There is no shortage of research ideas, but the key is to expand carefully and systematically into other research areas to increase your chances of winning proposals and to have fun during the learning process of discovering new research frontiers. A word of caution though: be careful with overcommitting yourself. I know I've mentioned that before. There may be a price to pay for too much success if your work–life balance is affected negatively. But who knows—maybe you are one of those who wants to achieve superstar status at all costs and with many awards in your closet!

THE NUMBERS GAME

The next most important part of the research portfolio is the number of students you support on your grants and contracts and how effectively you help them attain their degrees. Yes, administrators all over the country are hungry for the number of PhD students that departments can graduate per year, but do not get caught up in the numbers game. Do what is right! You may ask why the number of PhD students that a university awards is important. In the category of "Yes, we did this to ourselves," here is the answer: University rankings are based on the number of students graduated. Universities strive to reach worthy numbers so that they can be on these ranking lists with the hope that it will bring recognition and lure more students to their university. Take a look at some university websites. You will see that they proudly state they are ranked "insert whatever number here" for research ranking, or salary of graduates, or any number of things. At the end of the day, none of your students who graduate with a PhD are going to care about the ranking. They care about getting a good job and doing great research to discover new research frontiers. Therefore, you need to properly train and mentor students to succeed in their degrees and in their research. It does not matter that you graduate five PhD students per year if they cannot get jobs and are not making significant contributions to the field. In spite of all of these arguments, universities do expect you to graduate at least several PhD students before going up for promotion to full professor. Therefore, mentor and empower your students well, and your PhD numbers will speak for themselves without you having to obsess over the numbers game.

For graduate-only departments, the major goals are graduating MS and PhD students. I am often asked whether a student who finishes an undergraduate degree and wants to work on a PhD should be called a PhD student. I'll give you my thoughts. Not all departments and universities are the same. A student who has just finished an undergraduate degree may want to complete a PhD, in theory, but they are likely not mature enough to realize the rigors of graduate school. As a general principle, I suggest that students enroll in a Master's program to start. Then, at the end of two or so years, evaluate if they are ready to move to the next level of becoming a PhD student. Initial plans that are made right after graduating from an undergraduate degree will probably change. It is better that a student finishes the requirements of an MS degree and, if feasible, seamlessly moves to a PhD, moves to another university, or finds a place of employment than to struggle immensely and unnecessarily in a PhD program fresh out of undergrad. Being upfront about how the process works with a student at the very beginning will avoid confusion.

In departments where undergraduate degrees are being offered, it is truly a rewarding experience to get students involved in research very early on in their education. I am a firm believer that research at an early stage will help connect the courses better for student success, retention, and timely graduation. Research somehow provides purpose and direction for the undergraduate student. If you run a successful research lab, this is where you need to be careful about overcommitting, especially if you are a gifted teacher. When students take your class and get excited about your topic, they will begin to flock to your office to gain experience in your lab. Either find a way for the university to support a postdoctoral researcher to help you with this army of undergraduate students, or find support through grants, contracts, or private funding. Taking on too many students and not providing them the guidance on a day-to-day basis will only frustrate you and, more importantly, the student.

PUBLISH, PUBLISH, PUBLISH

No dossier is complete without showcasing your publications. You need to maintain an impressive number of publications each year. If you write several papers per year to be peer reviewed for high-quality journals (ignore things like H index for a minute) and if you help your graduate students and other team members write their papers, then welcome to another sweet spot in your dossier. I hope you are connecting the dots. As I've stated, you have to write several proposals to be successful. Then you build a team with graduate students and other researchers who will help you write a lot of papers and more proposals, which will result in your success. Then it is almost impossible for anyone in your university to say no to your promotion to full professor. Sounds easy, right? While it seems formulaic, it is hard work, and it is an approach that is rewarding across all levels: your students, your success, your promotion, and your contribution to your field. I call this a position of strength. It is also important at this stage of your career to take part in reviewing papers and also writing your own reviews for peers. It signals to everyone that you are an emerging leader in the field.

Let me get to H index and citation indices for a minute. Many universities and organizations are beginning to ask for such metrics with interrogative sentences such as, "It is not enough that you write good papers; how impactful are these papers?" In an age where the number of journals is exploding, you can start your own journal in a few weeks if you wanted. There are no regulations, governing bodies, or any such thing for monitoring this. However, your department should know which journals are the ones that are reputable and have a rigorous review process. These are the journals that you should be writing to so that people will read and cite your work. If you do good work and present your work at major conferences with high-quality publications in reputable journals, the rest takes care of itself. Do not get caught up in the numbers game of H index and citation index. Notice that people cite these indices depending upon which one gives them a higher number. The committees on campus that meet to deliberate your dossier will not go through rip-roaring discussions on your H-index "rating." I have been on all sides of that process, and I can easily say that if you prepare carefully with all the correct elements for promotion to full professor, you will do just fine!

THE SEMINAR

You need to be in the regular habit of carefully adjusting your travel schedule to give invited talks to universities and other organizations. If you are an emerging leader in your field, you should be getting invited to other universities and organizations to give seminars. Take these opportunities to stretch your skills, network effectively, and forge collaborations across universities. It shows your university and the rest of your community that you are not only a subject matter expert but also a team player.

Try this. Provide overview seminars in your own department (if they don't have a seminar series, organize one). If there is a seminar coordinator for your department, reach out and express an interest in giving a seminar. Early in your career, it is important for you to be a regular on the seminar schedule. Volunteer to give a talk every semester. Build your peer-reviewed paper portfolio and provide an overview of your discipline or your field of interest. Are there any interdisciplinary threads to your work? A physicist might give a talk in the mathematical sciences department to help form connections. Look at seminar opportunities across your college, and get connected with other departments. If you do not reach out, no one will know of your work.

TAKE-HOME MESSAGE

Research was critical before tenure, and it is just as critical post-tenure. Now is not the time to slack off. On the contrary, it's time to share your wealth of information with even more people.

JOURNAL ENTRY

Do you have a list of campuses you would like to visit to present your seminars? What about any institutions that aren't academic in nature?

FOOD FOR THOUGHT

It can be difficult to not obsess over numbers, after all, they are literally the deal makers. However, if you continue to genuinely dedicate yourself to carefully building and balancing your portfolios, you won't have to obsess; the results will show.

NOTES

SERVICE PORTFOLIO FOR THE ASSOCIATE PROFESSOR

21

The service component of your dossier should be strong as well. You should be moving away from "I need to check a box to fulfill my service requirement" and toward decisions that are more strategic in nature. I hate to put it this way, but the more colleagues you get to know in the next five years as you strive be a collegial colleague, a team player, and a future leader, the easier your case for full professor gets. Aim to serve on committees or ask to serve on committees that will add value to your understanding of the university. Try the College Promotion and Tenure Committee. You are now eligible since you are a tenured member of the faculty. If you are nominated, elected, and selected (yes, there is a process for that!), then it will be an eye-opener to see how different disciplines in your college work. Learn the process, do due

diligence, and don't be afraid to speak and engage in lively discussions. If you are really a glutton for punishment, serve on the faculty senate, where you will see firsthand how the business of shared governance takes place. If you thought the university was simply a business, then you'll get a kick out of seeing the political side of it. Have fun! Regardless, it is important to get to know your colleagues around the university as you serve in committees across campus. Keep this in perspective, though. You still have a lot of work to do in your research and teaching components. I have seen faculty members get carried away with serving on committees and seriously neglect their research and teaching. No one is going to promote you to full professor simply because you served on numerous committees, were collegial, showed up on time, and wrote reports. None of those things help the primary mandates of the university.

REVIEW PANELS

As an associate professor, your service to the research community is becoming even more critical. It is a given that you are reviewing papers and proposals regularly. Do yourself a favor and keep a database of all the proposals and papers you reviewed and for which agency. It will help with documentation if someone wants it! You never know when these things become useful.

It is absolutely imperative that you serve on review panels for funding agencies such as NASA, NSF, ONR, or DOE. If you get an email asking to serve on one, and if it is indeed in your area of expertise, do not turn it down. Do whatever it takes to adjust your schedule to serve on review panels. As your career matures, you can be more selective because the program managers who send the invitations understand that your responsibilities have increased. This is why it is important to seek out program managers in funding agencies at conferences to develop a network of relationships.

THE AWARD-WINNING ASSOCIATE PROFESSOR

It is important that you win a few awards along the way. If your research is breaking records, your department chair or colleagues should be nominating you for university and college awards. These are important as well. Depending on your discipline, the awards and the frequency of these awards vary. Do not stress yourself into thinking that you should become fellow of an organization at this point. A fellow of an organization is a stature attained after being successfully nominated for having won awards, having contributed largely to a field, and having produced publications. This comes with time or not at all. But winning meaningful awards during this phase is important. If no one nominates you for an award, don't be bashful. Send an email to a reputable colleague and ask them if they are willing to nominate you if you provide all the necessary information. I have had several researchers write me a note and ask me of my willingness to nominate them for the award. It has always been a privilege and an honor to do this since they were very deserving of these awards.

TAKE-HOME MESSAGE

You're teaching. You're researching. Don't forget to make sure that you are also serving. Those committees can have influence on university politics. If you want things around you to change, committees are a good place for your voice to be heard.

JOURNAL ENTRY

What award would you most like to be nominated for (and win)? Why? What can you do to help ensure that you are a candidate?

FOOD FOR THOUGHT

Good researchers are not just aware of what's going on in their bubbles; they also take note of other reputable researchers. Start paying attention to those you think would be great candidates for certain awards.

NOTES

YOUR SPHERES OF INFLUENCE

22

Now that I have piqued your curiosity with the title, let me explain what it means. When you first enter into a university, you probably have very little working knowledge about how a university operates. Understand that every person that you have communicated with thus far has their own perspective. Hopefully you carefully evaluated the department health and morale before entering into this journey (more on this later). The spheres of influence are the people who will affect you and those that you will affect.

1. **The early-career assistant professor who was hired before you:**
    The perspective of an early-career professor is useful, but be careful to not weigh one opinion heavily since your subject area of expertise

in that department may be different. Learn from her experience about expectations of the department and how the first year panned out. She can help you with navigating the purchasing system, the online learning management system, and office hours. Her student and faculty experiences may also be useful. Let me reiterate that it is not productive to get worked up about the department and university politics that you may hear from such individuals. Ask how she solved problems, which could be very beneficial so you do not have to reinvent the wheel! But realize that your experience may turn out to be different from the one that you are hearing from this individual.

2. **The senior professor who is eager to fold you under her wings:** Yes, you will encounter some aggressive personalities in your department who are eager to tap into your research expertise so that they can write more papers and proposals and in turn be even more successful. There's nothing wrong with wanting to be successful, but you need to be careful when engaging with aggressive types. If you do not figure out the rules of engagement about who will be the PI on a proposal or where you will end up on the coauthor list, you will get entangled in a difficult professional relationship. Start slowly but deliberately in collaborative relationships, and make sure that the quality of work speaks for itself. Remember that it is going to take time for you to set up your lab and your research program. If you overcommit too early in the process, you may not be able to deliver. Let me also provide some advice about collegiality. You may hear this word tossed around everywhere on campus, and people may even describe this as how nice you are. Be careful about getting too far ahead into social relationships with other professors. I know of a situation where a senior professor befriended a new early-career professor just for the purpose of gaining his vote at a faculty meeting. Sticky situations.

3. **Your graduate students:** These are the students that you work with on a near-daily basis. Of all the spheres of influence, this is probably going to be the most work yet also the most rewarding. These students expect you to train and mentor them in research and their careers. They are also looking up to you as someone who has been successful in navigating the multiple aspects of being a professor. Be prepared to spend a lot of time with them. Remember that your end goal is for them to conduct independent research. These students are part of your team, and your team is only as strong as the weakest link. It is your responsibility to make those weak links stronger!

4. **The students that you teach:** Your passion to teach the topic and how you care for your students, whether undergraduate or graduate,

is important. Some of you who have worked with children know this well. You can talk the talk but if you cannot walk it—your kids will call you out on it! Students are the same. You can wax poetic about how much you love to teach and mentor students, but if you do not teach competently, they will latch on to it. Be prepared, day in and day out!

5. **Your fellow faculty:** In most departments, things could get so busy that the only time you will see faculty is at a faculty meeting. Unfortunately, when these meetings are not conducted properly, they are a colossal waste of time. Plus, in contentious faculty meetings you only get to see the "bad side" of other faculty. All faculty should also be in attendance at department seminars (if there is no seminar series, start one!). But do not hold your breath; not all faculty show up for a variety of reasons. It is important for you to show up and stay engaged with the seminar series though. I am still envious of my colleagues in Australia where I took a one-year sabbatical. They got together for 20+ minutes in the morning at the faculty lounge to have tea and cookies (OK, biscuits for the Aussies who are reading this). And get this. They did it again in the afternoon for another 20 minutes. At the very beginning, I found it awkward and, to be honest, thought it was a waste of time. But looking back on it, it was quite useful to stay connected with fellow faculty. Ten years later, on some days I wish I had a cup of coffee in one hand and a biscuit in the other. Your faculty sphere of influence will interact differently based on where you are. Make the best use of it!

6. **Your mentor(s):** If you do not have one, this should be among your first priorities. Find a time where you can get away from your office (and his) and spend some quality time discussing your career path, opportunities, and questions you may have. If you can do this once a month, consider yourself fortunate. Good mentors should be competent, balanced in their viewpoints, and successful in their own careers. Sometimes departments assign mentors. If so, utilize their experience and advice. There is nothing wrong with having more than one mentor. But do not overdo it!

7. **Department chair:** Department chairs are busy people (most of them). I once knew of a department chair who felt that he had "arrived" and that he had to do very little and simply delegate. He rarely had meetings, showed up late for others' meetings, paid very little attention to students and faculty, and spent most afternoons having lunch with personal friends at various restaurants. How long do you think he lasted in his job? In my opinion, the job of a department chair is one of the most important on campus. In small to

mid-sized universities, department chairs continue to teach, mentor students, write papers and proposals, and also handle the administrative responsibilities. Hats off to them! They are sometimes the unsung heroes of the university. They are usually paid a stipend to carry out their administrative duties, which is often disproportionate to the amount of work required. You should at least check in with your department chair twice a semester. In the middle of the semester, discuss how things are going in research, teaching, and your assigned committees. You should also provide a wrap-up at the end of the semester to discuss challenges and how you plan on addressing them. Having open communication on a regular basis with your department chair is very important as you move toward your mandatory tenure year. Your department chair must be your biggest ally. Remember that they went through a lot of work to hire you; therefore, they have a vested interest in seeing you succeed.

8. **The staff assistant(s):** You may have heard that it is the staff assistant who "runs" the department. You may also have heard that good staff assistants are worth their weight in gold. Whatever the worth of gold is these days, it is important that you have a professional and cordial relationship with them. Some staff assistants go above and beyond their call of duty to help faculty, staff, and students. This does not mean that you should walk up to their desk, hand them a stack of papers, and say that you want ten photocopies in an hour. Not every department tasks their staff assistants to photocopy papers. Just be aware of how things are done in your department. Make sure that you send polite emails, and don't be too pushy. Remember that they are probably handling multiple responsibilities.

9. **Office of sponsored programs:** These are the folks that are going to help you with preparing budgets and the proposal submission process. Again, having a professional, courteous working relationship is important. Your proposal may be due tomorrow, but if you have not given the OSP staff adequate time (in my book, at least a week) to go through your proposal and double-check everything, then you have no right to be pushy! I know of faculty members who think that theirs is the only proposal that is important and demand that they have the right to work on their proposal until the last hour before the funding agency deadline. It does not speak well to the time-management aspect of the faculty member's life.

10. **Faculty in other colleges:** As you move through your career, you will begin to interact with faculty from other departments and colleges at several venues. There are many opportunities to socialize